how to JUST GIVE IT TO GOD

how to JUST GIVE IT TO GOD

PRACTICAL ADVICE TO HELP YOU LEAN INTO GOD'S GRACE

Jodi Sixkiller Keith

How to Just Give It to God

Trilogy Christian Publishers A Wholly Owned Subsidiary of Trinity Broadcasting Network
2442 Michelle Drive Tustin, CA 92780

10 9 8 7 6 5 4 3 2 1
Library of Congress Cataloging-in-Publication Data is available.
ISBN: 979-8-89041-318-5
E-ISBN:979-8-89041-319-2

DEDICATION

This book is dedicated to my husband, Charles. Thank you for always encouraging me in everything. Thank you for your devotion and love. Thank you for the honest feedback, for helping with research, and for your guidance and suggestions throughout this labor of love. Most of all, thank you for just being who you are. I love you dearly.

To my daughter Baylie, thank you for designing the cover and pull quote artwork. As your mom, it means the world to me that you would want to use your God-given talent to create this beautiful cover. I love the meticulous nature with which you worked through the design and that the script is your handwriting; it adds a personal touch I will cherish forever. This labor of love is so much sweeter since you employed your design skills to glorify God and because we get to share your talent with all our readers.

Special thanks to my friends and family for serving as the first-line editors and content reviewers. You have been the best at championing me through this process, and I am so thankful for every one of you.

Tonya McClish

Justin & Tammy Gibson

Marsha Glenn

Paula Hall

Baylie Keith

Coury & Jonna Tucker

Ethel (Pee-Wee) Luper

Janie Gipson (my momma)

Paula Reed

Julie Ballew

Cindy Lattimore

Special thanks to my sister Paula for providing the title to this book through years of advising me to "just give it to God."

Special thanks to my buddy Scout for providing life lessons that resulted in some of the content for this book.

CONTENTS

Introduction

Some Days I Still Struggle

Do you ever find yourself struggling in your Christian walk? Are you fidgeting, flailing, or even failing in areas of your life that should be full of faith, forgiveness, and freedom? Are you hanging on to past hurts, wallowing in grief that seems to have swallowed you up, or finding offense in anything and everything without leaving room to extend grace to the other imperfect people in your life? Me too! At least, that's where I was when God asked me to write this book. Although I would love to say that I now have it all figured out, that simply isn't true. Instead, I learned through this writing process that this is a lifelong journey while we are here on earth. The good news for Christians is that God does not expect us to fidget, flail, or fail. But even when we do, even when we choose to take the reins and ride out this life by our own power instead of asking for God's guidance and wisdom, He is always there to step in and rescue us once again.

The Bible says that we must seek God's Kingdom and His righteousness *first*. What if we make a conscious effort to do just this one thing? This verse ends with a promise for those who do, "…and all these things will be given to you as well" (Matthew 6:33, NIV). This passage is a quote from one of Jesus' teachings, and the "things" He speaks of are life essentials such as food, water, and clothing. Jesus questioned the people, "Which of you, if his son asks for bread, will give him a stone? Or if he asks for a fish, will give him a snake? If you, then, though you are evil, know how to give good gifts to your children, how much more will your Father in heaven give good gifts to those who ask Him!" (Matthew 7:9–11, NIV). We are God's children, and just like we desire good for our children, God desires good for us. I don't know about you, but in my life, God has proven this time after time. Yet sometimes, I still find myself in the middle of a struggle. A struggle that I chose to fight on my own just because I didn't seek Him first and ask for the help I desperately needed.

As I said before, I don't have it all figured out, but I believe God is using my life as an example to help others choose a better path and rise above the struggle. It is my hope that by taking this journey together, we may both learn how to ***just give it to God!***

Chapter 1

Say What??

Have you ever been going through a hard time in your life, and when you finally get to that place of seeking advice from someone you love, you hear this: "You're just gonna have to give that to God." *Say what?* How do you respond to that? What thoughts are racing through your mind at that moment? If you're like me, it's probably something like this:

- How am I supposed to do that?
- How is that going to help me right now?
- I already prayed about it, and nothing is happening. God just isn't answering me.

Have you ever wondered, what if it *was* that simple? What if I could literally approach God directly with my problem and physically hand it to Him? Would I suddenly feel better about being told to "just give it to God?" The picture in my mind looks like this: I am a small child, maybe five or six years old. I walk up to Jesus, holding out a bundle of problems wrapped in a nice and neat package. As I approach Him, Jesus leans forward, smiling at me, and gladly takes the bundle from my outstretched hands. Then, I turn and skip away, carefree off into the sunshine. Isn't that beautiful? What if I told you that's *exactly* what God's word tells us to do? Let's take a look at what the Bible says about giving it to God.

"Come to me all who are weary and burdened, and I will give you rest."

Matthew 11:28 (NIV)

(Jesus speaking)

"Humble yourselves, therefore, under God's mighty hand, that He may lift you up in due time. Cast all your

anxiety on Him because He cares for you.”

1 Peter 5:6–7 (NIV)

“So do not fear, for I am with you; do not be dismayed, for I am your God. I will strengthen you and help you; I will uphold you with my righteous right hand.”

Isaiah 41:10 (NIV)

“Do not be anxious about anything, but in every situation, by prayer and petition, with thanksgiving, present your requests to God. And the peace of God, which transcends all understanding, will guard your hearts and your minds in Christ Jesus.”

Philippians 4:6–7 (NIV)

“Submit yourselves, then, to God. Resist the devil, and he will flee from you. Come near to God and He will come near to you.”

James 4:7–8 (NIV)

“For the kingdom of God is not a matter of talk but of power.”

1 Corinthians 4:20 (NIV)

As followers of Christ, the Bible is our instruction manual for life, and it stands firm on the “give it to God” principle for solving our problems. If we believe in God and that His Word is true, why do we find that so hard to do? Throughout this book, I hope to provide some practical instruction for those seeking to find relief from the burdens of life and who desire to walk in the freedom that can only be found by giving it to God!

~ CHAPTER CHALLENGE ~

Earlier, I shared a vision of myself giving it to God. Now it's your turn.

Close your eyes and picture yourself giving it to God.

What does that look like for you?

Write it down somewhere. Share it with a trusted friend. Revisit it often.

Chapter 2

First Things First

I can't rightly give advice about leaning into God's grace without addressing the topic of salvation. I mean, first things first…right? If you have already accepted the gift of salvation, you have my permission to skip this chapter but remember it's here as a great resource if you need help leading someone to Christ. Let's start with a few facts about getting saved. Then we will dig into God's word to fill in the gaps. Here we go!

- Salvation is given to you freely by a gracious God who loves you.
- He calls you! If you are curious, questioning, or seeking God, it's because He is calling you. The very fact that you are curious about Him is proof of that calling.
- Do not get hung up on the "traditions of men" (humans). Many of us are running this race and doing the best we can with the instruction we have been given. If you have experienced being hurt by someone in the "church," remember they are human too. Point toward God's word and place your confidence in what He says, not in the opinions of others.
- Come as you are! There are misconceptions out there that you have to "clean yourself up" for God; this is simply *untrue*! Salvation *is* God cleaning you up. He knows everything about you, and He still loves you. How cool is that?

Now that we have established the groundwork and cleared up some common misinformation surrounding salvation, let's talk about how to get saved. I will start by sharing my salvation story.

Tidbit of Truth

I almost didn't share this. In fact, it didn't even cross my mind until my husband said, "I think you should share your salvation story here." It's not awe-inspiring; there are no big theatrics. It isn't dramatic at all, but it's a "precious moment" in the story of my relationship with God, so I have taken his advice and decided to share it.

My salvation story began at the tender age of eight in a little country church in Sallisaw, Oklahoma. My family was not "religious." We didn't hop in the car on Sunday morning and head off to church together. In fact, at that time in my life, I didn't even really know if anyone in my family was saved. Hanson Baptist Church was a small country church located less than a block from my house. Sometimes, on pretty days, my cousins and I would walk to church. On other days, my Granny Sixkiller, a.k.a. Granny Six, my mom, or my Aunt Jackie would drive us over and drop us off. The church had a church bus route, and occasionally, we rode the bus. In fact, this church bus route, or rather, the driver of the bus, is one of the only reasons I went to church in the first place. Her name was Lahoma Ross. She may be the best example of servitude and obedience I have ever witnessed. *Every Saturday* of my young life, one thing I could count on, without fail, was that Lahoma Ross would be stopping by my house on that church bus to see if she needed to swing by and pick me up for Sunday school the next morning. It drove my dad insane. "Why?" you might ask. Because he knew she wasn't stopping at just inviting us kids to church, she would invite him too. I don't know if it was out of conviction or just out of respect for my elders, but for some reason, I couldn't say no to her. Even if I didn't feel like going to church, I would break every time and say, "Yes, please come by and pick me up." Now I know she was all a part of God's plan for my life.

I can't recall many details about the day I got saved, but I do remember how nervous I was at the thought of walking to the front of the church during the invitation. Many Sunday mornings leading up to this day, I chickened out. I would try to talk myself into it, but I just couldn't do it. I remember shaking and holding back tears as I raced down the aisle to tell the adult waiting at the front that I wanted to be saved. The adult led me through the prayer of salvation, and that was it. I felt relieved that I had finally found the courage to ask Jesus into my heart. I don't even remember if I told my family. Little did I know that over the next few years, I would learn a lot about leaning into and running to the arms of Jesus. He would literally become my rock and my salvation from the evils of this world on more than one occasion. He would carry me through the storms of life and become my best friend and confidant. Jesus would become *my* savior—saving me from my past and saving me from myself.

Choosing salvation is about so much more than the promise of eternal life. Jesus chose you. He loves you. He wants you to live in a relationship with Him so He can help you navigate *this* life. Salvation is not about regulation and condemnation; it is about faith, forgiveness, and a love so big that our human minds cannot comprehend it. If you feel like the world is crumbling around you and that even if a giant arrow were pointing to the right choice, you would choose the wrong one, Jesus already knows, and guess what? He loves you anyway. Choose to follow Jesus. What do you have to lose?

Jesus chose you.
He loves you.
He wants you to
live in relationship
with Him so He can
help you navigate
this life.

At this point, I'm hoping you are ready to say yes to a relationship with God. If so...*let's go!* If you're still unsure, read on. Maybe you will be more confident about your decision by the end of this book. For those that want to accept the free gift of salvation, I have good news. We can take care of it right this very second! If you're new to the Christian faith, you may have a preconceived idea about what it takes to get saved. Forget all of that. You don't need a ceremony or a believer with you to make it happen. Jesus not only knows your name, but the Bible says that He knows the number of hairs on your head! My point is that if you call upon His name, *He will hear you,* and *He will know your voice.* So, if you're ready, all you need to do is follow the instructions given to us in Romans 10:9–10.

"If you declare with your mouth, "Jesus is Lord," and believe in your heart that God raised Him from the dead, you will be saved. For it is with your heart that you believe and are justified, and it is with your mouth that you profess your faith and are saved."

Romans 10:9–10 (NIV)

In case you are new to this, let me summarize what you just read. Basically, by declaring "Jesus is Lord," you are acknowledging that you believe God is the creator of the universe and that He sent His son Jesus to rule over all of creation. For new believers, I understand how this is a tall order, but think about this: If you don't believe in a creator, how do you think the universe came into being? If not God, who or how? Think about the intricate fashion with which the human body functions, wild animals survive, the ocean knows its boundaries, and the planets rotate around the sun at just the right speed, distance, and angle to sustain life. Next, the Bible says to believe in your heart that God raised Him (Jesus) from the dead. First, it is important to understand that God is a triune being, with "tri" meaning "three." He is Father (God), Son (Jesus), and the Holy Spirit. This can seem confusing, but here is what you need to know for now: God is the creator. When sin entered and the world became corrupt, God manifested Himself in human form and became born of a woman, Mary, entering the world of creation as Jesus (God's son but also still 100 percent God). Don't get hung up on this. Remember, you believe He created the universe, right? Jesus came to teach us how to live in a relationship with God. He experienced all the things that sin causes us in this life. He faced the loss of a parent and the death of a friend. He was shunned. He was called a liar. He was wrongly accused. He was mocked, ridiculed, and bullied. He was tortured. He was anxious. He was tempted. He was hungry. He felt tired. He felt stressed. He was broken-hearted. *He was human*. He also knew that He would die a horribly painful death to save you and me from the wages of sin…which is eternal death. We can read the account of how Jesus dealt with every situation in His chosen humanity, yet He never sinned. He couldn't because He was to be the unblemished sacrifice that would cover all of our sins forever and ever. I challenge you to read about Jesus' life in the Gospels and get to know Him (In the New Testament of the Bible, the books of Matthew, Mark, Luke, and John are the Gospels). Read about the brutal details involved in dying by crucifixion. Study how prisoners were treated in those days, or better yet, go watch the movie *The Passion of the Christ*.[1] It will give you a great appreciation for what Jesus endured for YOUR salvation. He died for you, but on the third day, when His friends went to the tomb to anoint His body, it was gone. God raised Him from the dead, and the Bible teaches that He sits at the right hand of God (Mark 16:19). There is so much more to the story that you will want to go read first-hand, but this is the basic premise of what you are called to do to receive your free gift of salvation. Are you ready? Let's pray this prayer together:

Dear God,

I declare Jesus is the Lord of my life. I confess that I am a sinner in need of a savior. I believe that Jesus died on the cross to save me from sin and that You raised Him from the dead. I ask that You send Your Holy Spirit to guide me through this journey of salvation and to remind me that You are always with me. Thank You for creating me. Thank You for loving me. Help me be more like You, Lord.

Amen

Let me be the first to say, *Welcome to the family!* I am so proud of you, and I know that you just made God's day!

In the days and weeks ahead, pray that God will give you a thirst for His Word; and I challenge you to read just a little of your Bible each day, even if you only have a couple of minutes, and especially if you feel like you don't want to, *press in!* You just stepped into a battle for your soul, and the enemy isn't going to let you go easily. We will talk at length about him in the next few chapters, but just know that Jesus wins in the end, so welcome to the winning team! Jesus said, "I have told you these things, so that in Me you may have peace. In this world you will have trouble, but take heart! I have overcome the world" (John 16:33, NIV).

Finally, just remember that the enemy trembles even at the sound of His name, so if you find yourself in a dark place and don't even know the words to pray, there is power in simply speaking the name of Jesus.

~ CHAPTER CHALLENGE ~

You are saved!

Write down your salvation story—every detail.

When you are feeling defeated in this world, read it.

I wish I wouldn't have lost those missing details in my story. Let my story be an everlasting reminder that God may call you to share your story someday, and if so, I pray that you have every precious detail.

Chapter 3

Burdened & Broken

Do you remember the first few days after you gave your life to Jesus? Did you have butterflies in your stomach like you were carrying around this grand secret? Maybe it was my youth, but I remember feeling like I wanted to tell everyone and, at the same time, to hold on so tightly as if the source of my newfound joy could be stripped from my hands at any moment. A big part of me wanted to shout it from the mountaintops, but the reality of the situation was that I sat idle, just trying not to mess it up. I continued to walk through my daily life as usual. I held my secret close, basking in my new relationship with Jesus and awe-struck at how loved and cherished it made me feel. Don't you wish every day felt like that? I certainly do. The hard reality for most of us, though, is that while we know we have been internally rewired, our external circumstances remain the same. How are we supposed to walk in the fullness of God's love when our heart feels burdened and our life feels broken?

Let's revisit a verse from Chapter 1. It is a great verse for the burdened and broken.

"Come to me all who are weary and burdened, and I will give you rest."

Matthew 11:28 (NIV)

Do you know who said those words? It was Jesus. Jesus! Telling us to bring our burdened, weary hearts directly to Him, and in return, *He* will give us rest. Let's break that down because it seems so simple, but oftentimes we are so focused on our brokenness that we forget the simplest of instructions. For new believers, take this one to heart. I'm a veteran Christian who can still find myself walking through a season of darkness before I realize I have been trying to fix it all by myself instead of running to Jesus and getting my rest.

Last year, we got a new puppy. Soon after we brought him home, I noticed that if he got scared or hurt, he bolted toward me with his tail tucked and wedged himself between my feet while trying to crawl up my leg. He wasn't satisfied until I picked him up, snuggled him close, and said, "Is my baby okay?" When I said those soothing words, he was ready to get down and play again. I thought this was the sweetest thing and figured he would eventually stop doing it, but that hasn't been the case. He has now had his first birthday and is still afraid of the train whistle when we are outside. He still bolts to my feet, and thankfully he is a small dog, so I can still sweep him up into my arms and say, "Is my baby okay?" I think this is a beautiful illustration of God teaching me how to run to Him. Whether the threat is real or perceived, this is how we *should* run to Jesus. It's what He told us to do. He didn't say, "After you try to handle it all on your own and feel defeated, crushed, hopeless, and *broken*, you can come to Me with whatever is bothering you." *No!* We need to grab hold of this.

The Bible says, "Cast all your anxiety on Him because He cares for you" (1 Peter 5:7, NIV). Read that again. *All your anxiety*. Not just the great big problems, not just the problems for which the world cannot provide an answer or a fix; *all* of your problems. In fact, it doesn't even have to be a problem, but anything causing you to feel anxious. Have you ever stopped to think about all of the things you're feeling anxious about? If you're like me, the list can be pretty lengthy, especially when I find myself adrift in the great sea of this world and I leave Jesus standing on the shore. I let guilt and shame keep me from asking for God's help with the "small stuff," as if the Creator of the Universe has to prioritize which problems He will assist with today. In my humanness, I tend

I let guilt & shame
keep me from
asking for God's help
with the "small stuff,"
as if the
Creator of the Universe
has to prioritize
which problems He
will assist with today.

to place God inside boundaries that *my* mind can comprehend. Asking God to bring peace to my anxious heart seems selfish when others are walking through something much bigger. Please hear me when I say this, God cares about your anxious heart just as much as He cares about the big stuff, but we have a part to play in obtaining rest. We are instructed to approach Him, "Come to me…" (Matthew 11:28, NIV), and to hand it off, "Cast all your anxiety…" (1 Peter 5:7, NIV).

In the book of Jeremiah, it is written, "For I know the plans I have for you, *declares the Lord*, plans to prosper you and not to harm you, plans to give you hope and a future" (Jeremiah 29:11, NIV). Verse 12 goes on to say, "*Then* you will call upon me, and *I will listen to you*" (Jeremiah 29:12, NIV). Finally, in verse 13, the Lord says, "You will seek me and find me when you seek me with *all your heart*" (Jeremiah 29:13, NIV). I pray that you and I will grab onto this declaration and refuse to let it go. That not by our own strength but by the power of God's provision, we will seek Him with all our heart. If our mind can't comprehend His power, we also can't comprehend His goodness, His wisdom, or His love. How great is it that we serve an everlasting all-powerful God that cares about even the small stuff? A God that knows His plans for us, which are life-giving, ushered in on the wings of hope for our future.

Burdened and broken may be by-products of this fallen world we live in, but thank God we can find peace and rest by running to the arms of Jesus.

~ CHAPTER CHALLENGE ~

What are you anxious about today?

Make a list of all of the things that are causing your heart to feel anxious today. Lay your hands on your list or hold it in your hand as you pray this prayer:

Heavenly Father,

Thank You for loving me and caring about all of my problems, even my anxious heart. Father, I cast these anxieties upon You and ask that You hold me in your loving arms so that I may find peace and rest as Your will shapes my future. Father, Your word instructs me to be anxious for nothing but instead to pray about everything. Thank You for sending Your only son Jesus who died on the cross, so that I could be forgiven of my sins.

Amen

Now, crumple that anxiety-filled paper up and throw it away!

Chapter 4

Committed to Chaos

In a world full of chaos, how are we supposed to find peace? By definition, the word "chaos"[2] means a state of utter confusion. Am I the only one that can use this word "chaos" to describe some seasons of my life? According to mainstream and social media, the sky is falling. But if I listen to their chatter, it has been falling every single day of my life, yet it remains suspended above me as if to hide heaven from my view. Yes, we live in a world that operates on chaos. We are connected twenty-four-seven to—quite literally—everything. I love my technology as much as anyone, but I believe being accessible every hour of every day creates a culture of chaos in our lives that can become a crutch. Left unchecked, this electronic escape from the real world can hinder all our relationships, including our relationship with God.

I am of the age that I remember life before cell phones and social media. A time when the world was more mysterious, bad news traveled slowly, and things seemed simple. Oh, how my soul longs for those days sometimes. Don't get me wrong, technology is helpful, but I do think it is important to acknowledge its contribution to the chaos we feel in our lives. We are constantly inundated with news, weather, triumph, and tragedy. We hold it in the palm of our hand. We live in an unprecedented time where easy access to us is the expectation. My job, students, distant acquaintances, and social media followers have as much immediate access to me as my family. All they have to do is open an app, pound out a message, and click send. Like many other things in life, technology is good, in moderation. This lifestyle of constant connectivity, though, can create stress and anxiety in our already fast-paced lives. Finding an escape in social media, online gaming, or any other outlet that causes you to isolate yourself from real human interaction can cause you to neglect other areas of your life that need attention. Comparison and anxiety can creep in and cultivate a heart that is unable to bear the good fruit God is trying to grow in you. If you're feeling convicted, friend, hang with me. I have felt scolded with every word of this chapter.

In the fourth chapter of Mark, Jesus teaches the parable of the sower. In Mark 4:16–17, He teaches about the sower that sows his seed in rocky places. The rocky soil receives the seed, and the plant may even grow and flourish for a short while, but it will be unable to grow deep roots and will only last a short time before it succumbs to its environment. In Mark 4:18–19, He speaks of the sower who sows his seed among thorns, the soil receives the seed, and the plant begins to grow, but true to the nature of thorns, they consume the plant and choke it, so that it is unable to bear fruit. Verse 20 teaches that the sower who sows his seed in good soil will produce a mighty crop. In this parable, Jesus is teaching about the condition of a person's heart represented by the type of soil. The seed represents God's word. These passages teach that a rocky heart may receive God's word and even be joyous about it, but the condition of the heart is such that the plant formed cannot grow deep and develop strong roots. As a result of these shallow roots, when the rocky heart faces troubles or is persecuted for being a believer, this heart will quickly fall back into the old habits that got it searching for relief in the first place. The second point covered by these passages teaches about the thorny heart. A thorny heart may receive God's word and even begin to grow. Still, it can easily become consumed with the "...worries of this life, the deceitfulness of wealth, and the desires for other things..." (Mark 4:19, NIV). These distractions cause the thorny heart to shift its focus off of God, choking out His word and becoming unfruitful. So, how do we make sure our heart represents the "good soil"? We need to create habits that help us become consumed with God's word.

When I look back at my walk with God, I see times when I went through a season of rockiness. In this season, my heart was not sensitive to God. I still loved Him, but I wasn't feeding His word to my heart. I slowly drifted away to a point where I didn't consult with Him in prayer, I didn't worship, and I didn't make time to cultivate my relationship with God. Likewise, I have spent my fair share of time among the thorns, mistaking short-term comfort for blessing and not realizing, until the thorns began to choke out my ability to bear good fruit, that I had once again drifted from God's word.

Bitterness, resentment, envy, self-serving, and self-righteous attitudes are the fruit of a rocky heart. Distraction, anxiety, unhappiness, a feeling of helplessness, being fearful, and a general feeling of being unsettled are fruits of a thorny heart. Are you bearing any of these fruits? If so, it's time to take a good long look at your habits. Think about it like this: to keep soil in good shape requires tending. You have to fertilize it, feed it, water it, and pull some weeds. When left to its own devices without intentional care, the soil will become a perfect environment for the weeds to grow and make way for the thorns. As the thorns take root, they will rob your soil of nutrients needed to produce a good crop. The moisture will wick away, leaving your soil dry, barren, and hard. When the storms come, any good soil that remains will be eroded. This is where you have a choice. What type of soil do you bring in to fix the scars of erosion? I would like to say that every time the storms come, I run to God's word for my new dirt, and I fill those scars of emptiness, loneliness, hurt, anger, and fear with life-giving Scripture; I mean, that's what mature Christians are supposed to do, right? I wish I could convince my humanity of that. Many times, though, my humanity takes over, and I bring in soil full of rocks or thorns to fill those scars left by the flooding.

I look to the world for answers instead of turning to God's word and spending time in prayer. Deep down, my independent (and hard-headed) spirit just wants someone to sympathize with me, to tell me I am right to be angry, hurt, and bitter. Deep down, I want to wallow in my brokenness for a while. Let me tell you from experience that this is dangerous ground. Even as I confess this weakness to you, I realize that I need to create better habits in response to hardships and hurts in my life. I need to be more intentional in seeking out the good soil of God's word and letting Him fight my battles. I need to learn to tell the will of my humanity "*no!*" and fall into the loving arms of Jesus for the small stuff so that when the storm comes, I go to that place first instead of turning to this world to comfort my burdened soul.

The truth is, this fallen world we live in is overwhelming. Technology allows us to know all the tragic events happening in real time, sometimes watching them unfold right in front of our eyes. Add that to the fact that our social media is sometimes filled with heartbreak and tragedy that our friends, family, and even our distant acquaintances are all walking through. Some days, my feed is full of loss, brokenness, and strife. I feel the heartbreak of situations I wouldn't even know about if the person wasn't my social media friend because we rarely, or never, correspond in real life. While social media can be a great outlet for expressing those hurts and pulling together a community of believers to pray for needs, I can't be the only one who feels overwhelmed at shouldering all this pain alongside my friends. I feel empathy very deeply, and I have to remind myself *a lot* that God didn't call me to carry those burdens. This is where I am really challenged with giving it to God.

For this reason, I can't let myself camp out on social media. When I let my guard down and go to that place to find an escape, I am a depressed mess. Likewise, looking at someone else's "perfect" life through the lens of social media can also be dangerous to your mental health, especially if you fall into the trap of believing they never have problems because they choose not to post them. I am writing a book about a lifetime of struggles, but if you stalk my social media, you will not see it there. It's not because I am trying to appear to be someone I'm not; it's because I choose to keep some parts of my life private and share others with the world. Comparison is an evil tool that the enemy uses to knock you down. If you are struggling with sadness, comparison, anxiety, or fear, your soil has become thorny. Rip those thorns out with the word of God. Start pouring God's promises into your heart instead of the manipulating and confusing accusations of the enemy. Find Christian podcasts and listen to worship music, but mostly, read God's Word for yourself and let Him speak directly to your heart. Even if it is just a little each day, it will produce much better fruit for you than the time you spend scrolling on your social media feeds—I promise! Obviously, if you suffer from an anxiety disorder, you should seek help from a medical professional. When I speak of an anxious heart, I am not speaking from the shoes of a person with an anxiety disorder but the anxiety we all feel based on general life circumstances. Before we leave this chapter of chaos in our rearview mirror, let's look at some great truths from God's Word.

If you are struggling

with sadness, comparison, anxiety, or fear, your soil has become thorny. Rip those thorns out with the word of God. Start pouring God's promises into your heart instead of the manipulating and confusing accusations of the enemy.

"But the fruit of the Spirit is love, joy, peace, forbearance, kindness, goodness, faithfulness, gentleness and self-control."

Galatians 5:22–23 (NIV)

"A good man brings good things out of the good stored up in him, and an evil man brings evil things out of the evil stored up in him."

Matthew 12:35 (NIV)

"Do not be anxious about anything, but in every situation, by prayer and petition, with thanksgiving, present your requests to God."

Philippians 4:6 (NIV)

"My dear brothers and sisters, take note of this: Everyone should be quick to listen, slow to speak and slow to become angry, because human anger does not produce the righteousness that God desires."

James 1:19–20 (NIV)

"Finally, brothers and sisters, whatever is true, whatever is noble, whatever is right, whatever is pure, whatever is lovely, whatever is admirable—if anything is excellent or praiseworthy—think about such things."

Philippians 4:8 (NIV)

God did not design you to live a life of chaos. Jesus bore that cross for you and me. We need to be on guard against the circumstances of life that are trying to suck us into a life apart from God's blessing. Start creating habits that point you to God in the good times so that when the bad days come, you won't fall into a life committed to chaos but will instead run to the loving arms of Jesus and find rest.

~ CHAPTER CHALLENGE ~

Take a minute to think about the things in your life that are currently creating chaos.

Make a list of those things.

Pray about them, naming each one and asking God to show you how to create some structure in any of those situations you *can* control. For situations out of your control, ask God to give you wisdom and guide you as you navigate this chaotic season of life.

Chapter 5

Failure Isn't Fatal

Remember that puppy I told you about back in Chapter 3? He has learned what it sounds like when we open the entry door from the garage into the house. When he hears that sound, he comes running full-speed down the hallway, and if you're not paying attention, he can take a knee out pretty quickly as he jumps straight into your legs. It doesn't matter if I have been gone for five minutes or eight hours; his excitement and response to my return remain the same. This sweet puppy, who has anxiously awaited my return, now just wants my attention. He wants to play and spend time with me. I wish every time I heard Jesus calling, this was my response…but it's not. There have been long seasons of drought in my Christian life. I am ashamed to admit that there have been times when I couldn't hear God's voice or feel His presence at all. I've experienced seasons when I didn't spend time in prayer, I didn't read His word, and I didn't seek to cultivate my relationship with Him. I've also spent seasons just going through the motions. My prayer life was stale, consistently doing my duty to pray for others' needs and reverently asking forgiveness for my sin…even voicing thankfulness but not really feeling it in my heart. Looking back at this time in my life, it seems I was more of a taker of the blessings I had come to expect from a faithful God. I wasn't reading His word and meditating on it as I knew I should be.

Much like human relationships, I didn't just wake up one day and decide I was done spending time with God; it happened slowly, over time. Sure, at first, I felt a little convicted. I felt the tug of God wanting me to spend time in His word, worship, and prayer. I even had moments when I missed that closeness I had once experienced with Him. Eventually, though, that still small voice was overtaken by all the things of this world that I easily found to fill up my time and use up the energy I had set aside for

Him. The scary part is that before entering most seasons of drought, I can't pinpoint any particular reason why it happened. I wasn't mad at God. We didn't have a "falling-out," I wasn't consciously turning my back on Him. I just got busy, tired, distracted, indifferent, self-reliant, ______________ (fill in the blank). Oftentimes, seasons of drought start when things are going well, not when the world is caving in on me. Self-reliance can run rampant in a season of health, happiness, and plenty if you don't keep it in check. When we look at the world through the lens of comfort, we may not feel as pressed to cultivate our relationship with God. Of course, this is exactly when we should seek all God has for us so that when the storms come—and they will—we are decked out in the full armor of God and able to withstand any obstacle that the winds throw in our direction. Why, then, do so many of us find ourselves in the middle of the storm without shelter? If we know the answer is to run back to Jesus, why do we wander in the world of darkness, looking for the light switch we hold in our hand?

The other day, I came home from work, played with my puppy Scout for a little while, then sat down to write. Scout bolted to find the closest toy and bring it to my feet. He wanted all of my attention, and he wanted it *now*! When I failed to respond the way he wanted, he began to bark at me. It went something like this...bark—wait—bark—wait—run to find a different toy—bark—wait—bark—wait—bark...you get the picture. If I don't pay attention to him, he continues; *he is relentless!* I'm not talking about a cute little puppy bark either, as his bark is transitioning to an ear-piercing, loud, big-boy bark. I have found my limit to be somewhere around six or seven barks, after which I break! I either stop and play with him for a bit or try to pull double duty pinning his toy under my foot while I continue to work.

I wasn't *mad* at God.
We didn't have a
falling out.
I wasn't consciously
turning my back
on Him. I just got busy,
tired, distracted,
indifferent, self-reliant,
______ (fill in the blank).

This struggle to take his toy from my foothold seems to satisfy him for a little while. Do you ever try to suffice God's call with the same foothold I had on that toy? I do. In my busy life, sometimes I pull double duty in my prayer life. I pray while brushing my teeth, driving to work, or folding laundry. I'm not saying this is a bad thing every once in a while, but sometimes, I find it to be my regular prayer routine. I know God deserves more of my time and attention than being a side thought while running out the door to my next event. Still, if I am not intentional about cultivating time for my relationship with God, I can fall right back into this routine pretty easily.

Recently, while my husband was out of town for business, this scenario with Scout repeated for an entire week. Scout had figured out how to get his way, and he was *loud* about it. I began to think about Scout's behavior and my response. My heart is soft toward him...I love him. He has been home alone, awaiting my return for a good ten hours. Was it really my expectation that ten minutes of playtime would suffice ten hours of waiting? My physical presence wasn't enough. What he desired was my attention, my emotion, my love. How often are we running through our day, checking off our tasks like we would complete a connect the dots activity? We hit the ground running in the morning and send up a prayer on the fly. We intend to stop and spend some time with God, but every possible thing that can happen today... does, and before we know it, we are exhausted and can't wait to get in bed so we can get up and run that race again tomorrow.

Can I get 100 percent real with you for a minute? Sometimes, I wish God would just bark loudly at me (figuratively, of course) when I need to stop and pay attention to Him. I know this isn't how God works, though.

How do I know? Because in the book of 1 Corinthians, Jesus defines love like this:

"Love is patient, love is kind. It does not envy, it does not boast, it is not proud. It does not dishonor others, it is not self-seeking, it is not easily angered, it keeps no record of wrongs. Love does not delight in evil but rejoices with the truth. It always protects, always trusts, always hopes, always perseveres. Love never fails."

1 Corinthians 13:4–8 (NIV)

Right off the bat, we can see that my Scouty-boy lacks patience, *haha*, but God *is* love, and His capacity to love is so big that our brain just can't grasp it.

God *is* patient. Much too patient to bark loudly at me to get my attention. If I'm honest about it, I would get tired of that and probably not find it very lovely anyway, wouldn't you? God could command us to love Him if He wanted. After all, He is our creator and the all-powerful Creator of the Universe. But friend, that is not His desire. He desires a relationship with us. He wants our attention, our emotion, our love. He wants to be invited into our lives, to walk with us, to talk with us, to rejoice with us in the good times, and to comfort us through the bad. That's why we have free will. God loves us so much that, although He could command our love, pursuing a relationship with Him is still our choice. I have said yes to a relationship with God many times since the age of eight. Rededication over and over again was for my benefit, of course, not for His. Over the years, I can look back and see how God has faithfully walked with me through every season, whether I looked for Him or not. Have I fallen on my face? Yes! Have I continued to crawl through the mud and muck of life even though I know God

Have I failed in my
walk with God?
Yes! Yes! Yes!
And guess what?
I will probably fail
again before I finish
the race of this life.
But hear me when I
tell you...

Failure isn't Fatal!

is there to rescue me? Yes! Because in my humanity, I was too ashamed to grab ahold of God's hand so He could help me up. Have I failed in my walk with God? Yes! Yes! Yes! And guess what? I will probably fail again before I finish the race of this life. But hear me when I tell you…Failure isn't Fatal! Did you hear that? Speak it out loud—*"Failure isn't fatal!"*

In our relationships with humans, our failure can prove fatal, slowing the heartbeat of the union to an eventual stop that cannot be revived. But…God knows our heart, He made our heart, and Jesus said, "My sheep listen to my voice; I know them, and they follow Me. I give them eternal life, and they shall never perish; no one will snatch them out of my hand" (John 10:27–28, NIV). Aren't you glad that no one can snatch you out of God's hand? To fully understand this, we must understand the significance of what causes our struggle in the first place. In the book of Ephesians, Paul wrote: "For our struggle is not against flesh and blood, but against the rulers, against the authorities, against the powers of this dark world and against the spiritual forces of evil in the heavenly realms" (Ephesians 6:12, NIV). The fight we are in is *spiritual warfare*. Evil spirits are at work in this fallen world, and the evil one still has the freedom to tempt and harass us. He is the great deceiver, a manipulating force at work in this world, just waiting for us to stumble in our walk with God so he can attack us with guilt and shame. I have good news, though. When Jesus died on the cross, He disarmed the powers and authorities of the "unseen world." The enemy may tempt and harass you, but he has no power over you if you are a born-again believer covered by the blood that Jesus shed on the cross for you. Hang on tight to this truth because I can tell you first-hand that Satan and his army are master manipulators, and if you try to fight him with your own strength—you will fail. He is very good at making you believe he has power over you and can do much more than toy with your mind and emotions, but the Bible clearly states that is a lie. Grab hold of this truth, and learn the tactics of this spiritual enemy so you can fight back with the only thing that will win against him…faith!

The Bible tells us to put on the full armor of God so we can stand against the schemes of the enemy. Ephesians 6:14–17 explains the armor of God.

"Stand firm then, with the belt of truth buckled around your waist, with the breastplate of righteousness in place, and with your feet fitted with the readiness that comes from the gospel of peace. In addition to all this, take up the shield of faith, with which you can extinguish all the flaming arrows of the evil one. Take the helmet of salvation and the sword of the Spirit, which is the word of God."

Ephesians 6:14–17 (NIV)

What if we took this literally, and every day when we stepped foot outside of our home, we were worried about flaming arrows being hurled down at us from any angle? Do you think we would be sure to put on our armor before leaving the house? I'm not even kidding when I say I would probably wear mine inside the house too. But this spiritual battle is hard. It is easier to focus on an enemy we can see, touch, or feel. Or, at least, it is easier to be distracted by a physical enemy.

I have a note written in my Bible on this page that says, "The enemy uses four powerful tactics against us: confusion, lies, manipulation, and accusation." But God's Word tells us many times, "Do not fear." We can't forget that Satan is a created spiritual being who still answers to God. Remember, he has no direct authority over you, but if you forget to suit up in the armor of God, you will lack the only weapon to defend against his attacks. The war he wages against us is spiritual warfare. The more our minds are filled with God's promises and truth, the less susceptible our thoughts and emotions are to the enemy's tricks. The hard part is to get our will to line up with God's will—and this is almost impossible if you are not feeding yourself God's Word.

Now that we know what our weapon is, how do we put on the full armor of God? Salvation, of course, is the first step for a non-believer. For believers, read and meditate on God's Word. Pray and worship. Cultivate your relationship with God. Remember, we are soldiers in a spiritual battle, and as such, we must approach our relationship with God with the same dedication and drive that a soldier must have while training to defend his or her country. If you find yourself in a season of failure—*push through*! The enemy's voice is loud, and he will boldly accuse you. Much like my puppy…he is relentless. The evil one pushes his agenda and manipulates you into conforming to his plan. Learn to recognize *that* is *not* love, so *that* is *not God.* Fight back with Scripture and the truth of who God says you are. If you think you are too weak to fight, remember there is power in just speaking the name of Jesus.

I have sat in that dark place. I have believed the lies of the enemy. I have been tricked into being too ashamed to call out to Jesus for help. I have gone years wallowing in my brokenness and being fed the lies of the enemy that I am helpless, hopeless, and unworthy. I found myself in this place because I didn't put on my armor, and when the going got tough, I forgot who I was. Thank God that failure isn't fatal, but I can tell you from experience that it is very painful. Friend, put on your armor. Put it on when you are tired, weary, devastated, and hopeless. Put it on when you are joyful, hopeful, happy, and strong. Be ready to fight with the word of truth because I promise the enemy is ready, and he will hit you where it hurts the most. Don't let him knock you off your feet. Fight him with God's truth and run to the arms of Jesus!

Before we leave this chapter, let's look at some truth about who God says we are. Read these words, write them on your heart, and be ready to use them as your weapon against the evil invisible enemy of your soul.

"For we know, brothers and sisters loved by God, that He has chosen you, because our gospel came to you not simply with words but also with power, with the Holy Spirit and deep conviction."

1 Thessalonians 1:4–5 (NIV)

"See what great love the Father has lavished on us, that we should be called children of God! And that is what we are! The reason the world does not know us is that it did not know Him."

1 John 3:1 (NIV)

"Therefore, since we have been justified through faith, we have peace with God through our Lord Jesus Christ, through whom we have gained access by faith into this grace in which we now stand."

Romans 5:1–2 (NIV)

"In Him we have redemption through His blood, the forgiveness of sins, in accordance with the riches of God's grace that He lavished on us."

Ephesians 1:7–8 (NIV)

CHAPTER CHALLENGE

Do you feel like you have failed in some areas of your relationship with God?

Grab a sheet of paper and write them down.

Pray over them, asking God to help you through those struggles so that you may draw near to Him and put on the full armor of God.

When you pray, read those failures to God and give them to Him one by one as you ask Him to redeem you and forgive you in those areas.

Chapter 6

Snakes & Scorpions

One thing I am positive about is that this title grabbed your attention for one of two reasons.

1. You love reptiles and other creepy crawly things.
2. You cringed and got chills simply from reading the title of this chapter.

Well, regardless of which category you fall into…this chapter leans more toward the latter of the two, in both a symbolic and a very real way.

Life has taught me that you can learn anything when it is necessary, especially if you are personally affected or afflicted by it. Last year, we built a new house out in the country—*way out in the country!* I'm pretty sure, at least in my lifetime, that there has never been a home on our land. The woods were thick, and we had to clear a lot of trees and underbrush to start the building process and get utilities to our building site. While clearing out the brush, we uncovered a few baby copperheads. If you aren't familiar with them, copperhead snakes are poisonous snakes. We never found the adult, but where there are baby snakes, there is a momma nearby. My husband and I both grew up in the country, and we have a healthy respect for the snake. We hoped we never encountered the adult snake, but we weren't ready to call off the whole building project because we knew it was out there somewhere. And guess what? Most assuredly, there is more than one adult snake out in the woods that surround our house.

Oddly enough, one night near the end of our building process, we were cleaning up after the bricklayers, and I found a dead scorpion. It had been years since I had seen a scorpion. But I was a country kid, and growing up, we had them in our house from time to time. About a week later, I went over to the house to meet the guy that was installing all of our hardware (door knobs, cabinet pulls, closet rods, etc.). It was a hot, humid Oklahoma day, even at ten in the morning. Since we didn't have air conditioning yet, it was *hot* inside the house. While opening the front door, I said, "Hey, we can open both of these doors and get you some air flowing through here." As I headed toward the back door, he said, "Well, I started to do that, but when I opened your back door, the biggest scorpion I've ever seen greeted me…so I said nope and closed it back as fast as I could. I hate those things." We both giggled, and I opened the door to find the scorpion was nowhere in sight…that's two, in case you're counting.

The house was finished, and we moved in around the first week of August. I had long forgotten about the snakes and scorpions. Then about two weeks after we moved in, my faithful alarm rang at 5:15 a.m. I rolled out of bed, placed my bare feet on the floor, and shuffled through the darkness to my bathroom to start my morning routine. Still half asleep, I reached for the light switch and flipped it on. As light filled all the places and spaces that were totally dark just a few minutes before, I rubbed my eyes and made my way over to the sink to brush my teeth. Suddenly, my sleepy eyes caught movement in my glossy white sink…evil was stirring. I rubbed my eyes again as if hoping that when I opened them the second time, it would be gone, but it wasn't. There, stuck in my sink, was an adult scorpion. It gave me chills, my heart started pounding, and I began searching my mind for the answer to how I would possibly get this evil-looking creature out of my sink so I could get ready for work—keeping count? That's three. I began wearing shoes inside the house and suggested my husband and son do the same since scorpions blend well with our tile floor choice. Never would I have dreamed that between mid-August and mid-November, I would go to war with a scorpion infestation that would lead to the eradication of around eighty scorpions…yes, eighty…approximately sixty-five of them, inside my house. The rest I killed outside—climbing up my brick, hanging out on my porch, in my garage, and (after I got a little braver) I even went hunting in the backyard one night and killed about ten or twelve. Finally, when the weather turned colder, they seemed to have disappeared. I have only killed one this winter. I am cautiously optimistic, as summer number two in this house approaches, that the scorpion problem will not repeat itself.

Even though it has been months since I saw a scorpion, I remain scarred by the fear I dealt with during that season of life. I have adamantly changed my behavior about wearing shoes in the house. Scorpions are unpredictable; you never know where one might show up, and I do not want to step on one barefoot. Until I found the scorpion in my sink, I had zero fear of stepping on one in my new house. Why would I? But after that day, my behavior changed. I began wearing shoes while in the house. After the next one was found, I began to worry about blankets hanging off the bed or couch. The more I told people my scorpion story and heard about their scorpion encounters, the more uneasy I became with my unwelcome squatters. I was ill-equipped to fight this enemy. I could handle one or two a summer…but eighty? Really? I interacted with more scorpions in those four months than I had seen throughout my life up to this point. Everything about this was abnormal. I did the only thing I knew to do…I Googled it! I quickly found out that my little scorpions were nothing compared to those found elsewhere in the world. Still, this uneasiness inside me remained. My husband sprayed the yard, and I bought scorpion spray to use inside the house, essential oils to spray both inside and outside, sticky traps, and blacklight flashlights. I learned more about scorpions in two weeks than most people will ever know in their lifetime. For instance, did you know that scorpions glow under blacklight? I didn't, but I do now. In fact, I now have a few blacklight flashlights in the house, and one stays by my bed so I can shine it on my flip-flops before putting my feet down in the mornings. Once upright, I walk through my dark house, scanning all around with my blacklight flashlight for any sign of glow-in-the-dark creatures that need to be eradicated before I can carry on with my morning routine. This scorpion problem is a real and relevant problem. I must equip myself to deal with it to protect myself and my family from the painful consequences of the scorpion's sting. If we were dealing with a snake problem, I believe my response would be much the same. Learn how to fight them, change behaviors, take necessary precautions to protect myself and my loved ones, and find the courage to fight the battle for eventual peace.

I recently heard a podcast in which the speaker likened the trials or woes of life to a snake. If you have ever been in the presence of a poisonous snake in the wild, chances are, you fixed your focus on him. You probably matched your gaze with every move he made in an attempt to ward off any surprise attack he might decide to unleash upon you. The funny thing is, if you hadn't crossed paths with the snake, if he would have slithered by unnoticed, you would have avoided the unrest altogether. And, in most cases, that's exactly how it happens. The snake goes about his way, and that is that...

but sometimes the snake gets into your house, barn, yard, etc., and becomes a nuisance you have to deal with. The speaker in the podcast said that focusing on the snakes of life can steal the peace and joy that God has planned for you. She is so right!

How many times do we get distracted by the snake? Even when the snake is long gone, we recount the story. We gasp about the what if's; we allow our mind to take us to the deepest, darkest place we can imagine. We shift our focus to the snake and even change our habits because of that one time that the snake caught us off-guard. I encountered eighty scorpions in and around my house, and to this day, every time I walk to my bathroom, I check the sink. Out of eighty scorpions, do you know how many I found in my sink?...*one!* I can tell you from experience that scorpions trying their hardest to take up residence with you certainly will demand your attention. However, the problem is that the *fear of finding the next scorpion*, or all of the ones currently unseen, is so much *worse* than the reality of the one you just had to deal with. Fear can be maddening, consuming your thoughts and creating anxieties that may never come to pass. The fact is, we killed sixty-five scorpions inside our house, yet my husband and son refused to heed my warnings to wear shoes. My son even jumped over one in his hall-way, but none of us ever got stung. I toiled over them not wearing shoes, whether or not they were letting blankets touch the floor, and making sure I went to bed before my husband so I could shake out all the bedding before lying down. These little enemies were ruling my life and stealing my joy. I thought about my fight with the scor-pions constantly. I was restless at home, feeling like I needed to be looking for any that had made their way into the house. While away from home, I worried that

fear

can be maddening,
consuming your
thoughts and
creating anxieties
that may never

come to pass.

my puppy would get a hold of one, and I read all of the horror stories online about what could *possibly* happen if he did. Sometimes, after lying in bed, I would swear something was crawling on me, or I felt like something had stung me.

The mind is a curious thing, isn't it? If you are old enough to read this book, you probably have some things in your life that are trying to pull your focus off of God and onto the problem at hand—some snakes or (in my case) scorpions.

The speaker of the message I mentioned earlier said she visualizes her problems as actual snakes—she even calls them "snakes." By doing so, it helps her remember to fix her focus on God and ask Him to help her with the problem instead of focusing all of her energy on the problem itself or, in many cases, the perceived problem. Have you ever focused on a problem that became so big in your mind that it consumed every thought, word, and action of your life? Did you come out the other side of that season realizing that your fear of the "what if" was much bigger than the reality of the "what is?" Believe me, I have spent some time in this season, and my worry did not change the outcome one bit. What it did do, however, was succeed in stealing my joy and rendering me ineffective in my Christian walk. The only thing worse than a miserable human is a miserable Christian. If you are focused on the snake, you will become consumed with the problems of this fallen world, and it will be nearly impossible for you to be the faithful witness you have been called to be for God's kingdom. So, what are we to do when we are face-to-face with the snakes of life? Let's grab ahold of a few truths from God's Word about the snake.

"I have given you authority to trample on snakes and scorpions and to overcome all the power of the enemy, nothing will harm you."

Luke 10:19 (NIV)

(Jesus talking)

In Genesis 3, God cursed the serpent for his deception of Eve in the garden of Eden. If you're new to Christianity, this deception led to Eve and Adam both disobeying God when Satan appeared to Eve as a serpent and tempted her. This temptation led to the fall of all humanity to the evils of sin. From this point on, the word serpent is used in the Bible when referring to Satan, a.k.a. "the evil one." Snakes and scorpions are mentioned in the Bible as an affliction to the peace of mankind. Snakes are mentioned as biting, striking, killing, and injecting poison. Likewise, scorpions are only mentioned a few times but always with a negative connotation.

In order to be victorious in my battle with scorpions, I had to know the characteristics of my enemy. I learned about the types of scorpions native to Oklahoma, then explored further to discover their habits and behaviors. As Christians, we are called to be soldiers for God's kingdom. Whether or not you realize it, you were born into a spiritual battle, and just like any good soldier, you need to know your enemy's characteristics so you can train and prepare your weapons for the fight standing before you. So…who is our enemy? Satan was actually a beautiful angel created by God. However, Lucifer became prideful, and his splendor led to his fall. Lucifer, forgetting (or ignoring) that he was a created being, decided he wanted to be exalted among his peers and that he wanted to be God's equal. In his blog, "Who is Lucifer in the Bible?" Dr. David Jeremiah wrote, "Because of his pride, he fell from heaven's glory, was sentenced to the pits of hell, and his name was changed to Satan."[3] "His new name, Satan, means "adversary" because he became the enemy of God and all His people when he defied God."[4] From the first time we are introduced to Satan in the book of Genesis, he is referred to as *the serpent*. And, guess what, friend? He does not work alone; he has an army of rebellious angels fighting with him. The Bible describes Satan as a prideful liar that is subtle, deceitful, and crafty, walking around as a roaring lion seeking to devour all God created for good. He prowls about scheming to seek and destroy God's kingdom by deceiving God's people into a life of condemnation and shame, rendering them ineffective in this spiritual battle.

My battle with scorpions somewhat mirrors Satan's attacks on our minds. I was living in barefoot bliss in my new home until I found that first scorpion inside the house. Remember the one in my bathroom sink? That day not only changed my habits but it also changed my thought process as well. I lost my ability to feel safety and comfort in my own home. As I jumped into learning everything I could about scorpions, fear began to take root. The fear of someone in our family getting stung led my mind to become consumed with my war on scorpions. I couldn't rest. I was either actively looking for them or thinking about what I needed to do next in order to win this battle. Unlike the copperhead snake, which literally has the power to kill you, scorpion stings, while painful, only in rare instances will result in death. Still, I couldn't find how they were getting into the house, and that was driving me crazy. I found them in the hallway, living room, kitchen, in my bathroom, my bedroom, and in the garage. Essentially, they were on both ends of our house.

In my current circumstances, the scorpion was a

more immediate threat to my family than the much more deadly snake. I believe this is exactly how the evil one steals our peace. We are walking through life, and as long as everything goes as planned, we can overcome the small stuff pretty easily. I felt relieved after I got rid of that first scorpion, like I had saved us from the pain of its sting. It was long gone, and we would never have to worry about that again...but I never saw what was coming. Instead, as soon as I had gone two or three days without seeing one, I would start settling in and feeling somewhat comfortable again, just in time for the next scorpion to find its way in through a crack or crevice and catch me off guard. Some days, I would kill two or three before bedtime, and on those days, I was growing increasingly weary over losing this battle.

Do you feel that way sometimes? Do you ever feel like you are teetering on your breaking point, and if *one more bad thing happens...* you'll just lose balance and topple over the edge? I can visualize myself holding a tennis racket, and Satan is hurling scorpions my way; they are coming slowly at first, and I can swat them with my racket. As he picks up the pace, I have two rackets, one in each hand. I am a mean green tennis machine! When the scorpions are being hurled at me so fast that my two rackets cannot deflect them, I sprout another arm and racket, then another, and this continues until I have about six arms and rackets all working together to keep the scorpions from hitting me—*but I can't keep up that pace*. My body begins to tire (it's my vision, so I make sure I never get stung...LOL), and a few scorpions hit me in the face. I am growing so weary and tired, and just before I fall from exhaustion, I call out to God, and He reaches down and plucks me out of that fight. The million-dollar question is...why do I fight to the point of exhaustion and through the sprouting of six arms before I ask God for help? The Bible teaches us that *the Lord is our strength* and that He is *always* there in times of trouble. Do you ever do that with your problems? Something happens today, and instead of pausing to pray about it and ask for God to help, you decide to just handle this one on your own. Then the next day, something else happens, and you start working on that one, but then maybe three things happen the next day. If you're counting... that's five. Are you going to be hard-headed like me and have to clone body parts so you can keep swatting down your problems until they consume you, or you become so exhausted that you are forced to ask for help only after you have been stung—*or*—are you going to be smart enough to trust God when there is just this one thing?

Remember, Satan has no direct authority over us. He does, however, have the power to tempt and harass us. And, generally, he will wait until you are already fighting the woes of life with six rackets before he turns a molehill into a mountain and pushes you to your breaking point. A weak and weary Christian is his ultimate playground. He is an expert at watching and learning the things that wear on your heart. Satan can't read your mind, but he doesn't have to. He learns everything he needs to torment you through your own words and actions. We need to watch for signs of his presence as diligently as I looked for those scorpions, maybe even more diligently. He is sneaky. He is patient. He is manipulative. If he finds a crack or a crevice in your armor, he will wiggle his way into your heart and mind. Given the opportunity, he will wreak havoc not only on your relationships with people but also attack your relationship with God. So, how do we defend against Satan and his tricks?

1

Know your enemy and remember his tactics: confusion, lies, manipulation, and accusation. Be mindful and watch for attacks or opportunities for him to attack you in your daily walk. He is cunning, and just like the snake, he blends in well with his surroundings. Satan can mask his attack as hurt feelings, unresolved anger, pridefulness, doubt, shame, guilt, and unforgiveness. If these emotions are allowed to sit and simmer inside you, Satan can gain a stronghold and begin planting seeds of bitterness in the soil of your heart. He will water those seeds with self-reliance, confusion, comparison, and condemnation that can drive a wedge into your relationships and result in you turning away from God's plan and purpose for your life.

2

Strike fast. What I mean by this is that we must learn to quickly discern any feelings, emotions, or attitudes contrary to God's word. The quicker we put a stop to the sprinkling of those seeds, the faster we can repent and ask God to guide our steps so that the crack can be sealed up before Satan gets a chance to run through it. The Bible says, "We demolish arguments and every pretension that sets itself up against the knowledge of God, and we take captive every thought to make it obedient to Christ" (2 Corinthians 10:5, NIV). To be on guard against this invisible enemy, we must *take every thought captive!* This means to think before we speak, and when we choose to speak…to speak life-giving words. We must also think before we react. We must be on guard and take captive thoughts that are envious, hurtful, negative, corrupt, and self-serving. We all have them. It's what you choose to do, or not to do, with them that can either set you up to win the battle or open a crevice for Satan to sneak in and set up camp. He will do it quietly at first. The torment will be slow because, remember, he is patient. All he has to do to make you an ineffective Christian who cannot bear good fruit is start using that unresolved negativity you have been storing against you. He will plant the seed and all that negativity you have been hanging on to will provide just enough water to start growing his crop of shame and condemnation.

3

Remember who you are, and more importantly, remember who your God is! The Psalmist wrote: "God is our refuge and strength, an *ever-present help* in trouble. Therefore, we will not fear, though, the earth give way and the mountains fall into the heart of the sea" (Psalm 46:1–2, NIV). This verse reminds us that God is *ever-present*. He never leaves us! We also read in the Psalms, "The Lord is my strength and my shield; my heart trusts in Him, and He helps me" (Psalm 28:7. NIV). In the book of 2 Samuel, we find this truth: "It is God who arms me with strength and keeps my way secure" (2 Samuel 22:33, NIV). Yet another great verse about who we are in Christ is found in the book of 2 Corinthians, "God made Him who had no sin to be sin for us so that in Him we might become the righteousness of God" (2 Corinthians 5:21, NIV). This verse right here sums up everything you need to remember about who God says you are. Let's recap. God sent Jesus, who was sinless, to be a sin sacrifice for you, me, and all believers that came before us and will come after us. Jesus gave up His life, paying the ultimate price for sin (death) so that you and I could *become the righteousness of God.* Have you ever wondered how we can be sinners yet be free from guilt or sin? It's because Jesus died on the cross to make us righteous before God! I don't know about you, but left to my own devices, righteous is not one of the words I would use to describe myself.

I hope these three steps will help you in your spiritual battle. I can say without reservation that I am forever thankful for my Savior Jesus and that He carried the weight of my sin to the grave to be buried forever under a cloak of mercy and grace. I am thankful that He rose from that grave—defeating death, hell, and the grave, and that He now sits at the right hand of *our* Father, the Almighty, the Most High King. When the enemy comes creeping around, throwing accusations and condemnation your way, remember who God says you are and remind that serpent and his friends that they have no power over you. We need only to stand on this truth found in the book of Psalms, "Whoever dwells in the shelter of the Most High will rest in the shadow of the Almighty" (Psalm 91:1, NIV). You are the child of the Most High King. Stick close enough to Him that you can find rest in His shadow. There is no better way to ward off an attack by the enemy than to dwell in the shelter of the King!

CHAPTER CHALLENGE

For this chapter challenge, I want to lead you through completing a word study so you can dissect your favorite verse.

My verse of the year is:

"Whoever dwells in the shelter of the Most High will rest in the shadow of the Almighty."

Psalm 91:1 (NIV)

Now…let's break down the meaning of each significant word.

(Google is a great help with this part, and I will give you a hint…type this into your search bar: "What does the word dwell mean in the Bible?" Then just change "dwell" for each word).

Whoever: Any person who.

Dwells: To live as a resident - reside.

Shelter: A place of covering or protection from violence, injury, annoyance, or attack.

Most High: God. Jesus is the son of the Most High. The Holy Spirit is the power of the Most High.

Shadow of the Almighty: In the presence of God.

Now let's rewrite this verse:

Any person who *resides* in the (*covering, protection*) of the *Most High* will rest in the *presence of Almighty God.*

What I learned from breaking down this verse into a common language is that I want to live a life close enough to God that I can find rest in His shadow.

Now, take this example and go break down your favorite verse. I challenge you to do this any time a verse speaks to your heart.

Chapter 7

Leaning In

"Trust in the Lord with all your heart and lean not on your own understanding; in all your ways submit to Him, and He will make your paths straight."

Proverbs 3:5–6 (NIV)

This same verse translated in the New King James Version reads: "Trust in the Lord with all your heart, And lean not on your own understanding; In all your ways acknowledge Him, and He shall direct your paths" (Proverbs 3:5–6, NKJV).

Quiet your mind for a few minutes. Think back to your earliest memory as a child. Now, drive your mind down memory lane from then until now. When those memories are good, envision driving on a four-lane divided highway with a big grassy median. It's a nice sunny day, and the road ahead is straight as far as your eyes can see... oh, and there is *no traffic!* Let's say you can comfortably and easily drive 80 mph on this road. As you encounter darker memories or small problems from your past, envision a curve in the road. Based on how painful or negative that memory is, you decide if the curve is significant enough to require a road sign to slow your speed. Was it a 50 mph curve? 45 mph? As your mind drives out of that negative memory, what do you see next? Did your road go back to that beautiful four-lane with no traffic, or when you navigated that curve, did you immediately encounter another? Then another? Were the curves getting sharper? Was the road narrow? Were your curves so sharp that they required a "dangerous curves" sign? Did they seem to stretch on for miles and miles with no relief? What other things did you encounter as you drove down memory lane? Potholes? Thunderstorms? Blizzards? Icy roads? Steep drop-offs with no guardrail? I don't know about you, but my drive down memory lane is anything but a four-lane divided highway on a sunny day with no traffic, and it sure isn't straight! In fact, in some places, my drive abruptly turns from asphalt to dirt with no warning. Throw in a little thunderstorm action, and before you know it—I am stuck in the mud...but I'm still here, friend, and *so are you!*

Last year when we were building our house, I would fly my drone now and then to capture construction progress photos. It's always amazing how even a little elevation changes the entire perspective of your view. In Chapter 6, I told you we moved way out into the country. Our property sits atop a rolling hill with thousands of mature trees surrounding it. Whichever direction you choose to look, you're only going to see as far as the thick wall of tree branches will allow, especially when they are leaf-on in the summertime. However, if I fly my drone 30–40 feet high, just above the treetops, something magical happens. Suddenly, there is a new perspective. I can see county roads that frame our property and jet off in all directions. I can see the railroad tracks nearby, my neighbors' yards, driveways, and rooftops. If I fly just a little higher, I can see the highway that's roughly four miles from my house, the lake that is about a twenty-minute drive away, and if there is a grass fire in the distance, I can see the plumes of smoke. From this high elevation, I can clearly see where the road is straight and where there are curves up ahead. But I can't see any of that standing in my driveway. If we know that God's perspective is better than ours, we should know the promises that He speaks over us. God spoke to Jeremiah, saying, "Before I formed you in the womb, I knew you, before you were born I set you apart" (Jeremiah 1:5, NIV). In this book, God also told His people, "For I know the plans I have for you." "...plans to prosper you and not to harm you, plans to give you hope and a future" (Jeremiah 29:11, NIV). Then in the book of Romans, Paul tells us, "And we know that in all things God works for the good of those who love Him" (Romans 8:28, NIV). Let's just camp out here for a minute. Number one: God knows you and me, and He knew us *before He formed us!* This doesn't mean that God only knew baby Jodi. It means that God also knows the Jodi I have yet to meet. Number two: God has a plan for our lives, and His plan is good. God doesn't desire for us to be harmed or for us to walk through this life only living up to the potential of our last mistake. He has a grand plan for you and me. Our problem is figuring out how to keep this sinful world we live in from distracting us. This world is full of issues that keep us from fully surrendering to God and tapping into His plan for us. Number three: He works in and through *all things* for our good. Sometimes, when our sunny highway quickly changes to a muddy mess, it's hard to see how God will use that mud for anything good. When I was at the height of my battle with eighty scorpions, I felt like I was living in a plague, not a blessing. Fast forward four months, and here's God using my scorpion story to minister to your heart. The fact is that God's view of my life is like that of the drone; He has a much better perspective than I do. I don't know what's coming, but I can take comfort in the fact that He does. When the dangerous curves of life sneak up on me, God will take the wheel—if I ask Him to—if I just *lean in.*

Remember how our opening verse ends? The part that says God will make our paths straight? I actually prefer the NKJV translation that says, "He will direct my paths" (Proverbs 3:5–6, NKJV). Why? Because in my drive down memory lane, my rearview mirror is full of treacherous and sometimes terrifying terrain. This sinful

I don't know whats coming but I can take comfort in the fact that He does.

world and spiritual battle sometimes get the best of me, and I begin to lean on my own understanding. Before I know it, I am back on the curvy road, and, unfortunately, sometimes, I can even find myself stuck in the mud again. If you're like me, aren't you thankful for a God that provides the best roadside assistance?

He pulls me out of the mud every time I call for help. He cleans me up and gets me back on the road. For a while, I may be back on that sunny four-lane, but I know I am high maintenance and may end up stuck or completely broken down again. I am keenly aware that I am being refined through the process, but I hope one day to find myself in that place where the curves, and especially the mud, are no longer roads I travel.

I don't want to wander in worry; instead, I want to fly by faith. I don't want to wade through the problems of life constantly on guard for the next blind curve up ahead. But when I wake up each day and choose to lead my life from my limited ground view instead of following the flight plan of faith, that's exactly where the road leads—e*very single time.* I know because I am an *expert* weary wanderer. I declare in Jesus name that I am going to do my best to put an end to this. I know it will require a new dedication to obedience on my part, and God will have to help me walk this out. He may even have to pick me up when I fall on my face again. Friend, if you are tired of trying to navigate the dangerous blind curves in your life, keep reading because I am going to share the plan God has laid on my heart to help me fly by faith in the arms of Jesus.

I am hanging on the promise that by choosing *every day* to trust God in, even the small stuff, He will direct my path. How am I going to do it? I am going to create some new habits. First, I am not getting out of bed without thanking God for getting me through the night and waking me up today. I know this sounds pretty fundamental, but remember, I said I want to practice trusting Him with *everything*. When I lay down at night—*I go to sleep*—haha. If I lay my head on my pillow before saying my nightly prayers, I will only make it through the first two or three thoughts. I won't even notice that I didn't finish the prayer until I wake up the next morning. Short of my dog barking or some loud noise or rare occurrence, I'm *not* waking up. For those of you that struggle with sleep, I realize this is a blessing, and I am not boasting—I'm making a point, I promise. While I am in my sleepy bliss, my lungs continue to take in oxygen and expel carbon dioxide exactly as designed. My heart continues to pump blood throughout my body. In fact, these things happen when I am awake too, without my worry, direction, or help. Could you imagine how ineffective we would be as humans if we had to command every breath? If to breathe, we had to have a conscious thought to breathe in—breathe out—breathe in—breathe out. Imagine yourself in an important meeting where you are trying to pay attention to details, or maybe you're the one leading the meeting, and you have to remind yourself every couple of seconds to breathe. Try to engage one of your friends or family in a simple conversation while consciously thinking, *breathe in, breathe out*. Even if you could do it successfully for a short time, it's pretty doubtful you could sustain it for twenty-four hours and still be productive with tasks that require your brain to engage. What if we physically began gasping for air every time we forgot? I would probably be passed out on the sidewalk somewhere in the first five minutes.

Have you ever just stopped to think of the precision

with which the body functions to sustain life without you consciously doing anything to help it? If this isn't proof of the Almighty Creator, I don't know what is. So, I am making a conscious choice to wake up each day and utter words of thankfulness to God for commanding my breath and for keeping my heart pumping throughout the night. I will ask Him to guide me in every step of my day and for Him to help me fly by faith over any obstacle I encounter today. I am going to create a habit of meditating on God's Word. I have chosen a verse of the year that has great meaning to me. I have been reciting it to myself as a declaration over myself and my family several times a day, and I plan to do this for the rest of the year. I actually shared my verse of the year with you in the word study at the end of Chapter 6. I am meditating on the meaning behind the words. If the process of speaking this verse every day becomes stagnant, I will go back to the word study and remember the power in this verse, and I will ask God to help me dwell in His shadow so I can find rest and be rejuvenated. I will be intentional in my prayer life, opening my prayer dialog with thankfulness to help me remember to speak of everything God has done for me. I will do this to create *in me* a grateful heart and to humble my human spirit to remember that without God's power—my body is unable to sustain life. I will seek every day to walk in obedience, no matter how big or small the task, having faith that God will equip me better than I could ever equip myself for the mission He has asked me to complete. Finally, I will hold God's Holy Spirit He has placed inside of me in such precious esteem that I will seek to hear and respond to His still, small voice. I will do this by being careful what I allow in through my eyes and ears. When my mind needs to be loud, let it be loud, singing praises to the one that deserves all of my time, attention, and love.

If you are struggling to stay out of the dangerous curves of life, or maybe you just keep finding yourself driving through a few minor storms, I invite you to practice "Leaning In" with me. As we finish this chapter, I want to provide a summary checklist of the steps I am taking to create a "Leaning In" habit in my own life. Feel free to use what works for you. I know this is very structured—but I also know myself, and this is exactly what I need!

1. Wake up with a thankful heart and speak that thankfulness to God before I even get out of bed.

2. Ask God to guide my steps and to help me fly by faith over any obstacles I encounter today.

3. Read God's Word daily and meditate on it throughout my day. For me, this meditation is my verse of the year, but meditating on any promise from God's Word will work. I will recite my verse to myself several times a day.

4. Be intentional in my daily prayers, offering them with thankfulness to create in me a spirit of humility and a grateful heart.

    If you are a brand-new Christian, start with those first four steps and progress as you feel ready. If you are a faithful believer who has been saved for a while, but you find yourself on the struggle bus like me from time to time, I challenge you to nail down the first four quickly and then move on to the final three steps.

5. Ask God for the courage to be obedient. We

are all called to be disciples. Not only to learn God's word but also to teach it to the lost and to use it to encourage other believers. God has equipped you with some kind of tool and following to do just that. Ask Him to reveal what that is, then take just the next small step in the direction of obedience. Even if your following is small, work on making an impact on those that God has placed in your circle. If you have a skill or talent (and we all have something), find some small way to glorify God with it. He can do more with your skill or talent than you ever could by your own power.

6. Cultivate your relationship with God by following the instructions given in the Bible to dwell in the shelter of the Most High so you can find rest in the shadow of the Almighty. Then sit back and watch Him work wonders with the plan He has for your life as you take one small step after another.

7. LEAN IN:

   - For the small stuff
   - For the big stuff
   - For the hard stuff
   - For the unfair stuff

   ...And don't forget to LEAN IN

   - For the good stuff

CHAPTER CHALLENGE

One sure way to fight off an attack of the evil one is to write God's word on your heart.

In this chapter challenge, choose a verse in the Bible that has great meaning to you. Just one verse. If you can't think of one or don't know the Bible well enough to choose one, here's some practical advice for you: Think of a word that means a lot to you this year. My word of the year is "Rest." I chose this word because I am walking out of a dark season where I have been distant from God. I have been weary, anxious, and burdened…I need *rest!* After choosing my word, I wanted a verse that kept the same theme of "Rest," so I went to Google and typed "Bible verses about finding rest" into the search bar. It didn't take long to find the one that spoke to my heart.

"Whoever dwells in the shelter of the Most High will rest in the shadow of the Almighty."

Psalm 91:1 (NIV)

Once you have selected your verse, write it down and strategically put it in places where you know you will see it every day. Every time you see your verse, create a habit of reciting it; if you think of your verse while away from your note, try to recite it from memory. If you will meditate on this verse, it won't be long until it pours out of you like common language. Once you have it memorized…move on to another one. By putting this simple activity into practice, when the enemy comes knocking at your door, you will have an arsenal of weapons (the truth of God's Word) to fight him with.

Chapter 8

Foundation of Faith

"Faith"...what a daunting word it can be. Especially when God asks you to walk in it for a season. According to the Oxford Languages online dictionary, "faith" is defined as a strong belief in God based on spiritual apprehension rather than proof.[5] I love the first part, but I take issue with the second part, and I will tell you why. First, I'm going to rewrite the definition, breaking down the word "apprehension" so you can see for yourself. In order to fully understand what this scripture is saying, we must understand the meaning of the word "apprehension." Apprehension has two definitions; first, it is defined as anxiety or fear.[6] A second definition for apprehension is: understanding or grasp.[7] If we simply rewrite the definition of faith, using each of these words to replace the word apprehension, here is what happens:

Faith: A strong belief in God based on spiritual anxiety rather than proof.

Faith: A strong belief in God based on spiritual fear rather than proof.

Faith: A strong belief in God based on spiritual understanding rather than proof.

Faith: A strong belief in God, based on spiritual grasp rather than proof.

I'm not sure which part bothers me the most, the fact that the world believes a "Strong belief in God" is based on spiritual anxiety or fear, that to have a "Strong belief in God," one must possess full spiritual understanding, or the fact that the world believes I blindly follow and believe in God with no evidence or proof.

In my opinion, the world's definition of faith is a near-miss. I much prefer the definition of faith in my Bible: "Now faith is the substance of things hoped for, the

In my life,
faith is often
found at the
intersection of
fear and
desperation.

evidence of things not seen" (Hebrews 11:1, NKJV). If faith is the substance, what does this mean? The Greek meaning of "substance" in Hebrews 11:1 is "foundation."[8] If faith is the evidence of things not seen, what does this mean? Evidence, by definition, is something that furnishes proof.[9] Based on this word study, we can conclude that your faith is *proof* that God is who He says He is, even though you cannot see Him with your own eyes. If you're worried that your faith is insufficient to be all the evidence you need of God's existence, sit tight—this chapter will set you free!

Let's go back to our word study of the Bible's definition of faith. *Faith* is the *foundation* of things hoped for, the *proof* of things that we cannot see. We know a foundation is a base for building all things. So, if faith is the foundation on which our belief system stands, how do we build our foundation of faith? I have good news: *we don't!* When you made a choice to follow Christ, and you asked God into your heart—at your salvation moment—God sent His Holy Spirit to dwell inside of you, and the Holy Spirit builds that foundation of faith for you. Galatians 5:22 tells us that *faith* is a fruit of the Holy Spirit. Faith, therefore, is not based on a feeling, emotion, or something we can see. Faith is evidenced purely in your belief that God is who He says He is and that His promises are true. God loves you and me so much that He even made a way for our belief in Him to be anchored to a foundation of faith built by His own Holy Spirit! God thought of everything. He is the master of details. Now that we no longer have to worry about how we obtain faith, let's take a look at how we exercise our faith or put it into action. While God so graciously supplies our faith through the power of the Holy Spirit, we do have a part to play in calling that faith into action. If you ever need a good reminder of some of the significant things in history that were accomplished by faith, just read the entire first chapter of the book of Hebrews. The words "by faith" appear more than fifteen times in thirty-nine verses!

Sometimes, the woes of this fallen world we live in require us to stand firm on our foundation of faith even when we don't think we can stand at all. Have you ever experienced a time like this in your life? I have experienced many of them. In fact, I learned about standing on faith at a very young age. You see, in my life, faith is often found at the intersection of fear and desperation—a place I found myself often in my youth as my family battled to survive my dad's drug addiction. At that intersection of life, it wasn't a fear of God that I experienced. Much to the contrary, it was the fear abounding in the circumstances of living in this fallen world that trapped me there.

In Chapter 2, I told you that Jesus would become my best friend and confidant—and I meant that with all my heart. I remember lying in my bed at night as a young girl, praying to God to take my mom away somewhere safe. This prayer still pours salt into a gaping wound in my soul. I remember bargaining with God…telling Him that I would be okay—even if I never got to see her again. I just wanted Him to take her to safety. I prayed fervently, standing on my foundation of faith and believing with all my heart that God would answer my prayer. I would like to say I bargained with God because of my youth, but the truth is, I have bargained with God in my prayers of desperation in my adult life too. I prayed that same prayer, night after night and year after year. Even as the hard days continued—I never wavered, as if one day I would muster up enough faith to save her. In my limited understanding, I thought there was a problem with my faith. Maybe I just didn't have enough; perhaps I just didn't believe enough that God would answer my prayer. I didn't understand that there were so many other variables at play here. And, I didn't understand that in these very moments of desperation, when I felt my faith was insufficient, God Himself was supplying my faith all along.

Eventually, my mom did get out, and while I didn't get to see her for a time, God did provide a way and a measure of safety for her. I am happy to report that my mom, the strongest woman I know, is still here with me today. While I may not understand the timing, I rejoice that God was faithful in answering my prayer to keep my mom safe. I also learned that when you are trapped in a situation over which you have no control, God hears your prayers of desperation. He supplies your faith through the Holy Spirit, and He is faithful—even when it seems like He isn't even there. Years later, I would find myself at this dreadful intersection again as I fervently prayed for my dad's healing. A prayer that God would answer in a much bigger way than I expected, but that certainly looked much different than what I was asking for.

My dad died at the age of fifty-one—a young man by today's standards. Years of uncontrolled blood sugars due to juvenile diabetes, coupled with his choice of lifestyle took their toll on his body. By the time he beat his addiction, in many ways, it had already beat him, and the five years clean provided him no reprieve from the thirty years of hard living that wreaked havoc on his body. His last year of life was spent in turmoil as he fought not only a spiritual war but also a physical one that would take his legs to the point that there was nothing left to take. Diabetes had taken his eyesight, and uncontrolled blood sugars had destroyed his kidneys too. He was experiencing a slow and painful physical death. But the hardest part, at least for me, was watching him sit in a very dark place apart from God's love and provision because he was so deceived by Satan that he couldn't see how God could possibly love him. The days of my dad's sickness are covered in my tears, heartache, and prayers. Prayers filled with confusion, as I struggled with even praying for the healing of a man who acted undesirable and voiced such ugly things at the mention of the name of my Savior. I eventually decided physical healing may not even come, and that's when my prayer language changed. I began to pray that God would find a way to save his soul.

When my prayer language changed, an odd peace filled my heart. It was as if God Himself was telling me to hold on a little longer because joy comes in the morning. As every surgery whittled away more and more of his body, I prayed fervently and desperately that God would soften his heart and send the right person to teach him about God's love. Even in his broken state, he was too prideful and hard-headed to listen to me or anyone else in our family. After eight long months in and out of the hospital and surgeries too numerous to count, he was told there was nothing else that could be done, and he made the decision to go home to live out his last days there.

On my dad's last day in the hospital, a nurse whom he dearly loved from his home health company came to visit. She was an older lady with a very small frame, and I didn't even know her name. I just know that she is my dad's angel. I may not remember all of her words to my dad correctly, but as she stood at his bedside, the conversation went something like this:

Dad (tearfully): They said there's nothing else they can do for me, so I guess this is it.

Angel Nurse (tearfully): I know Joe, they told me.

Joe, do you think I have taken good care of you and that I love you?

Dad: Yes.

Angel Nurse: Joe, have I ever lied to you?

Dad: No.

Angel Nurse: Okay then, I'm going to tell you something that might be hard for you to hear and even harder for you to believe, but I need you to remember how much I love you and that you said I have never told you a lie.

Dad: Okay.

Angel Nurse: Joe, God is real. Do you know Him as your Lord and Savior?

Dad (Sobbing, shakes his head softly back and forth as if to say no.)

Angel Nurse: Joe, it's true. God *is* real, and He loves you.

Dad (tearfully and softly): No.

Angel Nurse: Joe, listen to me. God loves you whether you want to believe that's true or not. He doesn't want you to spend eternity in hell when He has prepared a wonderful place for you in heaven.

Dad: There's no way He could love me.

Angel Nurse: Yes, He does!

Dad: You don't know what all I've done.

Angel Nurse: You're right, I don't know all you have done, but God does. He knows every deep dark secret that you have been carrying around all of these years.

And you'll have to believe me when I tell you that God loves you anyway.

At this point, I'm pretty sure everyone in the room was crying.

Dad: I can't believe He could love someone like me.

Angel Nurse: But that doesn't change the fact that He does love you, Joe. You don't have to understand; you just have to accept it. Are you ready to accept God's love?

Dad: Yes.

Angel Nurse: Are you ready to lay all this down and give your life to God, Joe?

Dad (sobbing): Yes, if you say He will have me.

Angel Nurse: Joe, do you think I would lie to you about the most important decision of your life?

Dad: No.

Angel Nurse: Well, I will pray with you right now, and we will ask God to save you if that's what you want.

Dad: Yes, that's what I want.

Angel Nurse proceeded to lead my dad through the prayer of salvation. The next day, my dad left that hospital for the very last time and went home to live out his last few days as a man saved by God's grace.

One thing I can say about my dad's fellow community of addicts is that they are faithful friends. They all showed up over the next several days to say goodbye to my dad. Those next two weeks after my dad got saved, he was happier than I had seen him in months. He sat up in his hospital bed, right in the middle of his living room, and told his salvation story over and over to a population of people that were walking that dark road he knew so well. People that, like my dad, had become a slave to their choices. A population that likely couldn't hear this message of love and hope from anyone else. I thanked God as I heard him repeatedly say, "You know how bad I am. If God can love me, He can really love you." A few weeks later, my dad left this earth for his heavenly home. His story is one of brokenness and heartache, but the Bible says, "The effectual fervent prayer of a righteous man availeth much" (James 5:16, KJV). And, I'm sure that while my Granny Six was going to church with her TV preacher on all those Sunday mornings, her heart was crying out to God to save her only son from the evils of his chosen lifestyle.

My dad tragically spent a lifetime seeking out things of this world, trying to fill a void only God's love could adequately fill. Nothing he chose satisfied that yearning inside. Instead, he was broken by a lifestyle that promised relief and an escape from the problems of life. He hurt so many people in the process and began to see himself as someone that was simply unloveable. Life tore him down physically, mentally, and, worst of all, spiritually. I find it very sad because underneath his chaotic disposition, my dad did have a good heart. I know because of the way he loved me and later, when he got clean from his addiction, the way he loved my daughter. He just fell victim to the lies and manipulation of the evil one. He played right into Satan's plan and walked a very dark road with him for a very long time.

So many things about being a drug addict's daughter were hard, but I can look back now and see God's faithfulness. He heard my prayers of fear and desperation and met me at that dreary intersection of life, providing a light—called hope—for my otherwise very dark path. When I could see no way, He *was* the way. And when my dad was standing at that same intersection of fear and desperation, He sent an angel in the only form my dad would respond to. That angel would help my dad find the faith to believe that God is bigger than his mistakes and that the blood of Jesus is sufficient to make even an outlaw like him not only lovable but also righteous in the eyes of God. Only God could have shown me the kind of love my heart needed through those difficult years. When I didn't know how to pray, He gave me words. When I couldn't find the strength to be strong for my dad during his illness, He sustained me. When I felt defeated because I couldn't see the evidence of my prayers being answered, He comforted me. And in the end, He not only answered my lifelong prayer that my dad would receive salvation, but He also allowed a time (that exceeded the doctor's expectations) in which I would get a preview of who my dad was truly created to be. The Joe Sixkiller I knew used his magnetic personality and charm to minister to the dark side during most of his earthly life. But in the sweetness of God, He provided a glimpse of the Joe Sixkiller I will walk with for eternity someday, and I can't wait to meet him again and truly get to know him.

Earlier, I told you that God would heal my dad, but it would look much different than what I was asking for. You see, I was pleading to God that He would heal my dad's broken physical body, and the truth is, He very well could have. I can drive myself crazy by combing over all of the reasons why the healing didn't come in the way I asked. Why he did or didn't deserve physical healing in his earthly body or why he wasn't able to stay here and live out his expected life span. I talked with God, at length, about this after my dad went to heaven, hoping for an answer that would heal the pain of my grief. Truthfully though, nothing could take away the pain in my heart at that moment. Even realizing that my dad was no longer in pain only provided temporary comfort for my sadness. But God knows we need that time to grieve in the midst of our sadness. If you cry out to Him, He is faithful to meet you at that intersection of heartache and despair in just the same way He met me a few times before in my battles with fear and desperation. I decided that I was either going to be consumed by grief or I had to shift my focus. Instead of focusing on the hurt of my loss, I decided to focus on all of the things about my dad's life that I was thankful for. After all, I was thankful for so many things. I was thankful that God had saved my dad; I was thankful that God had healed my dad, even if it didn't look the way I had planned. I was thankful that my dad died peacefully when he took his last breath, and the Holy Spirit filled that room so that there was no denying who my dad chose to live for those last few days of his life here. And, I was thankful that my dad not only got saved but also overcame staring death in the face to become a faithful witness for God in his last two weeks of life. In order to move forward, I had to go to God with thankfulness for these things and ask Him to repair my broken heart.

Choosing to follow God is not a promise of a life free from the trials and toils of this fallen world. My husband and I were recently discussing the spiritual battle we fight while on earth, and he said, "The truth is that none of us come out of this battle unscathed." He was so right. We are all warriors for the cause of Christ. We are going to be beaten up here because this world is not our home. Friend, your scars look different than mine, but one thing is certain, we all have them. As Christians, we have a hard time processing why bad things happen to good people. It's hard to serve a God who is good and still have to fight this spiritual battle. If we are going to live up to our calling, though, we have to remember our mission while on earth is, first and foremost, to love God and to love God's people. The last time I checked, we are called to love *every single human* God chooses to create during our short time walking this earth. I know this can be especially hard when people in your life are unlovely. I think it is easier to live out this mission if we remember three things:

1. Our time on earth is just a blink of an eye compared to the eternity we get to spend in heaven, living life the way God intended. So, hang on... eternity is coming!

2. This fallen world can be ugly and hard. It is full of heartache and despair. I sometimes think this is to help teach us what a life apart from God's provision looks like. It is exceptionally hard when bad things, unexpected things, or even tragic things happen to good people or maybe to us when we have been trying so hard to be faithful. We want to understand when sometimes, understanding isn't for the here and now. We have to remember that God does comfort us during these hard times. I believe His heart even breaks with and for us. On my drive to work each day, I try to remember that all of my students carry some emotional baggage into school with them on any given day. I try to remember that they are teenagers and that God has put them in my path for two reasons...to love them and to teach them. God taught me several years ago that regardless of our differences, if a student knows I genuinely care about them,

their future, and their problems, they truly become teachable in my class. Love conquers all.

3. Faith isn't something we have to produce, but it is freely given in just the amount needed by God's Holy Spirit that lives inside you. Remember little Jodi praying for her mom to be taken away to safety? In my Christian immaturity, I thought I didn't have enough faith for God to swoop down and save her. But my childlike faith kept me praying anyway in hopes that one day, God would hear my voice and answer my prayer. I now know God did hear me *every single time I asked*. And when my mom found safety, my ability to trust in my foundation of faith became stronger. The Bible confirms where, and more importantly, who our faith comes from in the book of Hebrews, "Let us throw off everything that hinders and the sin that so easily entangles. And let us run with perseverance the race marked out for us, fixing our eyes on Jesus, the author and perfecter of our faith" (Hebrews 12:1–2, NIV).

Aren't you glad that the Creator of the Universe meets you right in the middle of that dark and busy intersection of life? And, aren't you relieved to know the Holy Spirit is always there supplying the faith you need when you wouldn't have the courage or strength to be faithful by your own power? Let us not forget the Bible says that faith is our foundation of things hoped for, which means that when all you can see is a glimmer of hope in your darkest hour—that's faith! But take heart and know that on the days when you can't even see the glimmer, the Holy Spirit inside you is still providing a solid foundation of faith on which you can stand, and it is made perfect by fixing your eyes on Jesus!

CHAPTER CHALLENGE

Do you keep a praise journal?

Not a prayer journal but a *praise journal*?

I recently bought a new planner, and it has a column labeled "prayer" and a column labeled "praise." As I began to use my new planner, I realized the value of separating the two. My prayers begin with thankfulness but often end in petitioning God to fulfill my needs. Praise, on the other hand, is purely thankfulness and gratitude with intentional recognition of God's provision. A praise journal sometimes seems futile because you may think there is no way you will ever forget how God delivered you from this! But just let a little time pass and see if you can clearly recall all of those answered prayers.

For this Chapter Challenge, I challenge you to start a praise journal for you and your family. Dedicate a notebook or journal and try to make a goal of each day just jotting down answered prayers or circumstances in which you know God had His hand of protection on you or your family. Encourage other members of your family to write their praise reports in the journal as well. A year from now, you will be able to look back and see all of the times God was faithful. If you already keep a prayer journal, I challenge you to separate the entries for prayer and praise so you can clearly see answered and maybe even unanswered prayers.

Chapter 9

Focus on ~~the~~ *Your* Father

In the last chapter, you got a small glimpse of my life as Jodi Sixkiller. Though there were many good days in my life, those memories are quickly overshadowed by the hard ones. There's just something about the memories that cut deep into your soul with such authority that they take your breath away. Those memories...they're hard to forget. Life can be confusing when the world seems to be crumbling right under your feet as you're grasping at this and that, just trying to keep from falling into that never-ending pit of fear and heartache.

I often wonder what my life would be like if my story would've been different, if my dad had been a man of God in my formative years, teaching me to trust love instead of to fear it. Let me be clear, I never suffered physical abuse at the hands of my father. I know he loved me, and I knew it then. But, his drug-induced rage unleashed upon my mom was emotionally and mentally exhausting to me. Fear, anxiety, and confusion were trying their best to take me out. Obviously, my earthly father was broken, and I am not alone. According to the National Center on Substance Abuse and Child Welfare, "In the United States, about 1 in 8 children ages 17 or younger are living in households with at least one parent who has a substance use disorder."[10] To put this in perspective, the largest public school in my state averages approximately 870 students per grade level in grades 9–12. That means there are potentially 110 students *per grade* in grades 9, 10, 11, and 12 that fit this demographic. What a staggering statistic! Isn't it heartbreaking to think that in an English class of twenty-four students, three of them are carrying that emotional baggage into school *every single day*? And these are only the statistics for substance abuse. These numbers do not consider all of the other types of abuse that children in the United States are dragging around in their emotional suitcases. If you're still in high school and reading this book, think about that the next time you walk into your English class. Do you have an idea of which three kids this could be? Is it you? If you've long left high school in your rearview mirror, stop for a moment and think back. Can you pinpoint any kid in your class that may have been carrying this baggage? I can tell you from experience that the weight of the secret is heavy. And if I'm being honest, it was pretty hard to see that God had my best interest at heart while I was walking through that fire. The hard truth is this life is a battle for all of us. Your story may not include a drug addict parent and domestic violence, but I can almost guarantee there is something hard you have had to walk through. Maybe you're walking that dark road right now. I wish there were some magic fix I could reveal to make it all better. Unfortunately, on this side of heaven, they don't exist short of God intervening with a miracle. In my mom's case, God did intervene with a miracle—it was my Granny Six, my dad's mom. My Granny Six was brave enough to make my dad leave town while she strategically helped my mom escape. I will never forget hugging my mom goodbye, standing in my Granny's driveway. Sad yet relieved, I now wondered if I should have told God that it would be okay if I never got to see her again. But I stood on my foundation of faith and found hope that He would keep her safe and reunite us someday.

I know there are many stories like mine that, tragically, have a different outcome. I just want to take a minute to say that I'm sorry. I truly am. I'm sorry that you are walking through the fire or that you cried out to God for a rescue or healing that didn't happen the way you planned. Friend, that's so hard, and I sympathize with your pain. I will be the first to admit that when the pain

All I could really
process in that
moment was that
I felt powerless
to stop the pain
train as it barreled
through my broken
life.

is so deep that I can barely breathe, the last thing I feel capable of is giving that to God. Do you feel this way too? As if your heart is crying out: "This pain is *mine!* This problem is *mine!* I cried out to you, God—I trusted you, yet here I am burdened and broken (and maybe it ends with the most tragic word of all)...*again*!" I have walked through that fire. I have found my feelings hurt when I questioned why God didn't miraculously rescue me at that moment, even as I cried out to Him over and over again. What I have learned, though, is that God *was* there. I just couldn't see Him from my current perspective, standing in my Granny's driveway or hiding in my closet, consumed by fear. In fact, all I could really process at that moment was that I felt powerless to stop the pain train as it barreled through my broken life. I couldn't see then what is so blatantly obvious now. My mom, my granny, myself, and countless others were wounded casualties in my dad's spiritual war. In the aftermath, I can see why God sometimes had to carry me through that darkness. You see, in order for my dad to open his heart to God—*he* needed to walk through the fire. God could see the bigger picture of my dad's salvation, but believe me, I was not thinking about that when I was focused on surviving the moment!

God has been faithful to use my broken life as a testimony, and this book has definitely been an opportunity for me to reflect on my most painful memories. Throughout this process, I have found myself asking the million-dollar question…where was God in all of this? If you get nothing else from reading my story, I hope you get this: *God was always there,* whether I looked for Him or not! In fact, in my young faith, I didn't even really know what I was looking for. What was the evidence of God in my life? You may be wondering the very same thing. As

I reflect on my life, I can now see where God placed *His* people in my story at just the right time to fulfill a purpose.

Do you remember in Chapter 2 when I told you about Lahoma Ross, the church bus driver that would show up every Saturday? I believe with all my heart that God will credit a good portion of my salvation to her obedience. In my more mature Christian walk, I have learned that, oftentimes, God uses His people very strategically to walk alongside us. To be our battalion of sorts, providing the support we need as we fight our battles. And, if we aren't looking for God in those people—in those moments—we will miss Him.

Here's a small glimpse of how God used some of His people in my life. In elementary school, I became best friends with a girl named Chalon Looper.[11] The Looper family is so deeply woven into my memories of young Jodi. In fact, most of my good childhood memories were made with the Loopers, hanging out at their house or on trips with them to the lake. I spent a lot of time at their home, and one summer (at the height of my dad's drug addiction), I think I may have even lived with them. The Loopers were so important to my life in ways I wouldn't know until much later. They provided a glimpse into a family of normalcy for me. I'm sure they had their flaws, but through my lens of brokenness, they seemed pretty perfect to me. I watched them love their kids unconditionally through failures and successes. I observed Stanley's love for his wife, Modell—it was kind, fair, and beautiful. Probably most importantly, I experienced the parental love I was craving through them. They lovingly corrected me when I was wrong. They celebrated my wins. They taught me how to "night fish" and ride a four-wheeler. My friend even taught me how to swim at their house. The Loopers were good godly people, and they even took me to church with them. I owe a debt of gratitude to Modell and Stanley; they will forever hold a special place in my heart. They had a choice to look the other way, to simply not get involved. But they chose to love, and like Lahoma Ross, I believe a portion of my salvation will be credited to them. If anyone in the world modeled God's fatherly love for me in this life, it was Stanley Looper.

By the time I reached ninth grade, my mom and dad had been separated for a year and a half, and I was living with my Granny Six. This is a great time to tell you that my Granny Six is an amazing woman and really deserves her very own book. I miss her dearly and can't wait to walk and talk with her in heaven someday. Anyway, this is when I would meet the boy I would fall in love with forever! My dad was living about three hours away, and my mom was living an hour away in the opposite direction. Life was calm for a season. Meeting and falling in love with my now-husband would introduce me to two more men that would become so important in helping me begin to comprehend God's fatherly love for me: my husband's grandpa (Poppa Willie) and my father-in-law (Charles). These two men made me feel so loved and valued at a time when my dad was off battling the demons of his addiction. After my husband and I married, I became really close with my father-in-law, who treated me like a doting father. He would truly value me as his daughter until the day he went home to be with the Lord late last year. You see, as God weaved my story together, responding to choices made by the key players in my life, He placed His people strategically, each with a part to play—to help me in every time of need.

"Even to your old age and gray hairs I am He, I am He who will sustain you. I have made you and I will carry

you; I will sustain you and I will rescue you."

Isaiah 46:4 (NIV)

God is real to me because He has rescued me so many times. As a child, my life was full of uncertainty born of circumstances beyond my control. As an adult, I can look back and see where God clearly carried me again and again. Yet, in my humanity, I still struggle with trust and fear sometimes. Does my story sound similar to your relationship with your earthly father? Maybe for any number of reasons, you didn't have a father figure in your life at all. If so, let's learn together about the characteristics of our Heavenly Father, and let's take a look at why we should fix our focus on Him. Even if you had the best father that this world could possibly supply, your flawless Heavenly Father is capable of so much more. How wonderful that your earthly father gave you a great jumping-off point to truly be able to better grasp the magnitude of God's great and perfect love.

"See what great love the Father has lavished on us, that we should be called children of God."

1 John 3:1 (NIV)

If you've been a Christian any length of time, chances are you have read this verse or even sung it in a song. Have you ever really paused for a moment to think about the gravity of this particular verse? By now, you know how I love word studies, so let's break this one down! In this translation, I believe the most overlooked word is "lavished."

Lavished: To bestow something in *generous* or *extravagant* quantities on.[12]

Bestow: To present an honor, right, or gift.[13]

God is real
to me because
He has rescued
me so many times.

Now let's rewrite the verse:

"See what *great love* the Father (God) has *gifted in extravagant quantities* upon us, that we should be called children of God."

You and I have got to grab hold of this truth! Basically, God loves you so much that He has gifted you His great love in extravagant quantities. Not only has He given you His great love, but He also knows you as His very own child! Do you know what this really means? You are the child of the Most High King. The Bible calls us a co-heir with Jesus Christ Himself! Remember this the next time the evil one tries to tell you he has dominion over you. You turn right around and remind him that darkness cannot exist in the light, and your Father is the light of the world. If you are a parent, this word study probably hits you a little harder. Maybe you are thinking about how much you love your own children. If you don't have children of your own, perhaps you have nieces or nephews that you love more deeply than any love you have ever given before. If you dream of having children of your own someday, but you're just not there yet, think about the feelings you have for the person you love most in this world—believe it or not, you will love your children even more than that! I know it is hard to imagine, but it's true. Jesus addresses parental love in the book of Matthew: "You parents—if your children ask for a loaf of bread, do you give them a stone instead? Or if they ask for a fish, do you give them a snake? Of course not! So if you sinful people know how to give good gifts to your children, how much more will your Heavenly Father give good gifts to those who ask Him" (Matthew 7:9–11, NLT).

Wow! We are sinful and imperfect as humans, aren't we? Yet the majority of us strive to be good parents to our kids, even though our humanity has a way of rearing its ugly head sometimes. You know from reading Chapter 8 that my earthly father was obviously flawed. Even so, I knew he loved me. He even doted on me the best way he knew how in his broken state. I love how this verse reminds us that, as humans, we are all flawed. We are all sinners. Sure, the sin of some is more blatantly obvious and far-reaching than others, but we all have it. Then in the very next verse, we are reminded that there is one who is perfect, who doesn't just practice love as an emotion, but who *is* the very definition of love. And the best part is—He is our Father. To really put this verse into context, I think of my dad and how even in his brokenness, he wanted good for me. Then I think about my husband and what a great, wonderful, godly father and leader he is to our children, how he prays for them and asks God to place a hedge of protection around them. He is patient; he is kind; he is understanding and approachable. He wants good for them in everything they do, and he is great at communicating that to them. Even if he doesn't understand, he tries to be supportive of their ventures. He is wise counsel when they need advice, and he is who they turn to when they have problems they can't fix themselves. He makes everyone laugh, and most importantly, he is genuine—what you see is what you get. Even though he is by far the best father I have ever witnessed in this life, he is still limited by his humanity.

The truth is God's love for us is far better than anything we can think or imagine. The Bible says in 1 John 4:19 that even our very ability to love is only made possible because God loved us *first*. I know this life can be hard sometimes, but I do not believe that God causes bad things to happen to His children. We are victimized by our own spiritual battle, and oftentimes we are wounded casualties in the spiritual battle of others in our lives. I truly believe that when we find ourselves in that dark place, the only answer is to focus on our Father. Not our imperfect earthly father, but our Perfect Heavenly Father. The Creator of the Universe. The Creator of you! Before we leave this chapter behind, I want to share a tidbit of truth with you:

"For we are God's Masterpiece. He has created us anew in Christ Jesus, so we can do the good things He planned for us long ago."

Ephesians 2:10 (NLT)

Yes, friend, you are God's masterpiece. I pray your earthly father is a great reflection of your Heavenly Father, but even if he isn't, set your focus on the Father of Creation, The Most High King, your Perfect Heavenly Father, and take heart in knowing:

- He knows your voice.
- He hears you when you call.
- He has good things planned for you.
- He is always with you.
- He will never leave you.
- He will never forsake you.
- You cannot be plucked out of His hand.

And most importantly...know your rights!

"Yet to all who received Him, to those who believed in His name, He gave the right to become the children of God."

John 1:12 (NIV)

You are a masterpiece crafted by the best artist. He knows everything about you—the good and the bad—and He still loves you with a love so intense that we cannot even fully comprehend it. Aren't you glad that God loves us as His children? That He is proud of us when we accomplish great things? That His heart breaks when we are brokenhearted? That He is wise counsel and a listening ear when we need help? And, aren't you glad that when we can't walk through the fire, He carries us?

Friend, if you haven't accepted the free gift of salvation, are you ready to live your life for God? Are you prepared to lay your burdens at the feet of Jesus and choose a life focused on your Heavenly Father? If so, I urge you to go back and prayerfully reread Chapter 2. For my brothers and sisters in faith, I encourage you to be steadfast in the height of the battle. Lean into God's promises, and trust your faith so you can find freedom in living a life focused on your Father!

~ CHAPTER CHALLENGE ~

For this chapter challenge, you need to reflect on your life a bit.

When you take that drive down memory lane, take note of the people you now know God strategically placed in your life to help you through a season of uncertainty, discouragement, failure, heartache, etc.

Take the time to jot those names down in a notebook or journal, along with a short description of the role they played in your life.

Are they still in your life?

Do you know where they are now?

Take a moment to pray for the people on your list. Thank God for sending them when you needed them the most. Acknowledge His good work in your life through the people He sent to show you His love for a time.

Chapter 10

Just Give It to God

"But the Lord is faithful, and He will strengthen you and protect you from the evil one."

2 Thessalonians 3:3 (NIV)

Well, it's time to bring this journey to an end. I hope that you have found encouragement and motivation and maybe even worked through some of your own misgivings as you have read and resonated with my story. I started the journey of writing this book out of blind obedience. I was on the cusp of a spiritual attack on my mind and emotions that had gone on far too long. The enemy had succeeded in rendering me ineffective in my Christian walk, and he seemed to be winning. Then, one day, I walked into the living room and asked my husband to pray over me...that this darkness would be gone from me. He did. We talked about some habit modification, such as *not* listening to true crime every single day to and from work and all other times I needed to escape the chaos of my thought life; instead, finding good, fruitful, godly things to fill my heart and mind with words of life and encouragement. These things seem so obvious now, but in the weariness of my battle, they were lost on me. Maybe I just needed to hear someone else say it. I know these good habits work, so how did I get so focused on the negatives of life that I ended up here, burdened and broken?

I knew something had to change, and I was desperate to shake this funk I was in. So, I made these changes to my routine and focused on rebuilding my prayer life. I found Sadie Robertson Huff's "WHOA, That's Good Podcast"[14] and made myself listen to it for a week instead of true crime. Believe me, it was hard. I didn't realize how much I relied on this habit of listening to true crime until I tried to stop. But at the end of the week, I found that I couldn't wait to learn who Sadie's next guest would be and to soak up the godly wisdom they would impart. I have actually gone back to her first episode from 2018 and listened to them consecutively over the past few months. I began wanting to dive back into reading God's Word. For the first time in years, I found myself encouraged, motivated, and at peace with who God created me to be instead of fearful, suspicious, and weary of everything around me.

A few weeks later, while folding laundry and listening to worship music, I heard God's voice in my head telling me to get my prayer journal. I admittedly ignored it at first, but then I heard it again—"Go get your prayer journal." I went to retrieve it from my bedside table and opened it up to see that my last entry was written in 2015, eight years ago. I had many entries. I tried to write down everyone I prayed for back then and a short summary of their needs. I flipped through page after page and thought about where those people are now and what I know or don't know about their lives. I wondered if they saw the fruit of answered prayers. It was reassuring to see names written and needs I know God has since met. Friends that I helped pray through a season of divorce who are now living a restored life in a healthy relationship. Those that were healed of illnesses and those that I helped pray through tough life or business decisions that are now enjoying the fruit of those successes. Some of the names in my journal have gone on to heaven now, perhaps receiving the ultimate healing we will all desire when this earthly body no longer functions as designed to sustain life in this world. After thumbing through my prayer journal and feeling convicted about how stagnant my prayer life had become, I wrote down the date and jotted down the names and needs heavy on my heart. I laid hands on the names and asked God to meet their needs for whatever was being requested. I closed my journal and went back to folding laundry. It wasn't long until my mind began to wander, and I heard my sister's voice as clear as a bright sunny day saying, "You're just gonna have to give that to God." I was taken aback—where was this coming from? I heard it again, and there was no mistaking it was the voice of my sister, Paula. Paula is ten years older than me and, in many ways, she is more like a mom than a sister. At any rate, there was no mistaking her voice nor that piece of advice I had heard from her many times in my life, sometimes even echoed in passing. My mind was immediately filled with the questions that open Chapter 1, penned there because as soon as I heard my sister's voice, I immediately heard God say, "Go pick up your pen." I admit He had to tell me a couple of times as I tried to bargain with Him that I am no author, but I obeyed, and chapter one was written in the next hour or so.

I was catapulted back to that moment of salvation when I was eight years old. That feeling of having this great secret that only God and I knew about. Then, about an hour after I finished writing Chapter 1, I anxiously announced to my husband, "Ummmm, I think God is asking me to write a book." His response was everything I needed at that moment—loving, encouraging, and motivating. He said, "We should pray over it," so we did. I have been writing this book for a little over two months, but I now see that God has spent forty years prepping me for this moment. It has purged my soul and brought about some hard truths in how I can be better at pursuing my own relationship with God *at all times*. I have worked full-time, worked my side hustle as a photographer, raised a teenager, battled COVID a month ago, and even as I write this chapter four weeks later, I am home recovering from pneumonia. But God. He is faithful. His grace and provision are always sufficient to complete the good work He has started in us.

I really didn't know what God was up to when we started this journey. He gave me words when I sat down to write, or He didn't. If no words came, I took that as a sign that He wanted me to rest on those days. I figured since I was walking in obedience, I would trust His message and His timing. I pray that as you have read through each chapter, your story or the story of someone close to you is what played in the movie theater of your mind. I pray that the truth of God's word, woven through some of my hardest moments, provides healing and hope if you're currently walking through some dark and dreary days. I pray that you will use this book as a resource and turn to it when you need to be reminded that God is always there. I pray that in your weakest moments, you will remember that there is power in simply uttering the name of Jesus!

In true teacher fashion, I feel as though this chapter needs to be a chapter of reflection. One that you can quickly turn to when you find yourself or a friend struggling and need to grab a quick bite of God's living word. After all, Jesus is the bread of life, so isn't He the superfood we need to fuel up with for the fight? Let's go!

REFLECTIONS
&
RESOURCES

CHAPTER 1: SAY WHAT?

The Bible stands firm on the "give it to God" principle for solving problems. Find freedom by learning to "just give it to God." Let's review some of the truth from God's Word on the subject.

"Come to me all who are weary and burdened, and I will give you rest."

Matthew 11:28 (NIV)

(Jesus speaking)

"Humble yourselves, therefore, under God's mighty hand, that He may lift you up in due time. Cast all your anxiety on Him because He cares for you."

1 Peter 5:6–7 (NIV)

"So do not fear, for I am with you; do not be dismayed, for I am your God. I will strengthen you and help you; I will uphold you with my righteous right hand."

Isaiah 41:10 (NIV)

"Do not be anxious about anything, but in every situation, by prayer and petition, with thanksgiving, present your requests to God. And the peace of God, which transcends all understanding, will guard your hearts and your minds in Christ Jesus."

Philippians 4:6–7 (NIV)

"Submit yourselves, then, to God. Resist the devil, and he will flee from you. Come near to God and He will come near to you."

James 4:7–8 (NIV)

"For the kingdom of God is not a matter of talk but of power."

1 Corinthians 4:20 (NIV)

CHAPTER 2: FIRST THINGS FIRST (Salvation Chapter)

- Salvation is given to you freely by a gracious God who loves you.

- He calls you! If you are curious, questioning, or seeking God, it's because He is calling you. The very fact that you are curious about Him is proof of that calling.

- Jesus is not only the Savior of the World—He is *your* Savior. He desires a relationship with you, not a religion based on rules and regulations.

- Come as you are! Salvation *is* God cleaning you up. He knows everything about you, and He still loves you. How cool is that?

- Choosing salvation is about so much more than the promise of eternal life. Jesus chose you—He loves you. He wants you to live in a relationship with Him so He can help you navigate *this* life.

"If you declare with your mouth, "Jesus is Lord," and believe in your heart that God raised him from the dead,

you will be saved. For it is with your heart that you believe and are justified, and it is with your mouth that you profess your faith and are saved."

Romans 10:9–10 (NIV)

CHAPTER 3: BURDENED & BROKEN

- How are we supposed to walk in the fullness of God's love when our heart feels burdened and our life feels broken?

- The Bible says, "Come to me all who are weary and burdened, and I will give you rest" (Matthew 11:28, NIV). This passage is Jesus—telling us to bring our burdened, weary hearts directly to Him, and in return, *He* will give us rest. Oftentimes, we are so focused on our brokenness that we forget the simplest of instructions.

"Cast all your anxiety on Him because He cares for you."

1 Peter 5:7 (NIV)

- Not just the great big problems, not just the problems for which the world cannot provide an answer or a fix...*all* of your problems. In fact, it doesn't even have to be a "problem," but rather anything causing you to feel anxious.

"For I know the plans I have for you, declares the Lord, plans to prosper you and not to harm you, plans to give you hope and a future. Then you will call upon Me, and I will listen to you. You will seek Me and find Me when you seek Me with all your heart."

Jeremiah 29:11 (NIV)

CHAPTER 4: COMMITTED TO CHAOS

- Being accessible twenty-four-seven creates a culture of chaos in our lives that can become a crutch and, if left unchecked, can hinder all of our relationships, including our relationship with God.

- Bitterness, resentment, envy, self-serving, and self-righteous attitudes are the fruit of a rocky heart. Distraction, anxiety, unhappiness, unsettled, fearful, and a feeling of helplessness are all fruits of a thorny heart. Are you bearing any of these fruits? If so, it's time to take a good long look at your habits.

- Create better habits in response to hardships and hurts in your life. Be more intentional in seeking out the good soil of God's word and letting Him fight your battles. Practice telling the will of your humanity "*no!*" and fall into the loving arms of Jesus for the small stuff—so that when the storm comes, you go to that place first instead of turning to this world to comfort your burdened soul.

- God didn't call us to carry all the burdens of this world's problems.

"But the fruit of the Spirit is love, joy, peace, forbearance, kindness, goodness, faithfulness, gentleness and self-control."

Galatians 5:22–23 (NIV)

"A good man brings good things out of the good stored up in him, and an evil man brings evil things out of the evil stored up in him."

Matthew 12:35 (NIV)

"Do not be anxious about anything, but in every situation, by prayer and petition, with thanksgiving, present your requests to God."

Philippians 4:6 (NIV)

"My dear brothers and sisters, take note of this: Everyone should be quick to listen, slow to speak and slow to become angry, because human anger does not produce the righteousness that God desires."

James 1:19–20 (NIV)

"Finally, brothers and sisters, whatever is true, whatever is noble, whatever is right, whatever is pure, whatever is lovely, whatever is admirable—if anything is excellent or praiseworthy—think about such things."

Philippians 4:8 (NIV)

CHAPTER 5: FAILURE ISN'T FATAL

- I didn't just wake up one day and decide I was done spending time with God; it happened slowly, over time.

- Eventually, though, that still small voice was overtaken by all the things of this world that I easily found to fill up my time and use up the energy that I had set aside for Him.

- I wasn't mad at God, we didn't have a "falling-out," I wasn't consciously turning my back on Him…I just got busy, tired, distracted, indifferent, self-reliant, ______________ (fill in the blank).

- Oftentimes, seasons of drought start when things are going well, not when the world is caving in on me. Self-reliance can run rampant in a season of health, happiness, and plenty if you don't keep it in check.

- When we look at the world through the lens of comfort, we may not feel as pressed to cultivate our relationship with God.

- Why do so many of us find ourselves in the middle of the storm without shelter? Why, if we know the answer is to run back to Jesus, do we wander in the world of darkness, looking for the light switch that we are holding in our hand?

"Love is patient, love is kind. It does not envy, it does not boast, it is not proud. It does not dishonor others, it is not self-seeking, it is not easily angered, it keeps no record of wrongs. Love does not delight in evil but rejoices with the truth. It always protects, always trusts, always hopes, always perseveres. Love never fails."

1 Corinthians 13:4–8

"My sheep listen to my voice; I know them, and they follow me. I give them eternal life, and they shall never perish; no one will snatch them out of my hand."

John 10:27–28 (NIV)

"For our struggle is not against flesh and blood, but against the rulers, against the authorities, against the powers of this dark world and against the spiritual forces of evil in the heavenly realms."

Ephesians 6:12 (NIV)

- The Bible tells us to put on the full armor of God so we can stand against the schemes of the enemy.

"Stand firm then, with the belt of truth buckled around your waist, with the breastplate of righteousness in place, and with your feet fitted with the readiness that comes from the gospel of peace. In addition to all this, take up the shield of faith, with which you can extinguish all the flaming arrows of the evil one. Take the helmet of salvation and the sword of the Spirit, which is the word of God."

Ephesians 6:14–17 (NIV)

- If the armor of God is our weapon, how do we "put on the full armor of God?" Salvation, of course, is the first step for a non-believer. For believers—read and meditate on God's Word. Pray and worship. Cultivate your relationship with God.

- Remember, we are soldiers in a spiritual battle, and as such, we must approach our relationship with God with the same dedication and drive that a soldier must have while training to defend his or her country.

- If you find yourself in a season of failure—*push through*!

- Put on your armor. Put it on when you are tired, weary, devastated, and hopeless. Put it on when you are joyful, hopeful, happy, and strong. Be ready to fight with the word of truth because I promise the enemy is ready, and he will hit you where it hurts the most. Don't you let him knock you off your feet. Fight him with God's truth and run to the arms of Jesus!

"For we know, brothers and sisters loved by God, that he has chosen you, because our gospel came to you not simply with words but also with power, with the Holy Spirit and deep conviction."

1 Thessalonians 1:4–5 (NIV)

"See what great love the Father has lavished on us, that we should be called children of God! And that is what we are! The reason the world does not know us is that it did not know Him."

1 John 3:1 (NIV)

"Therefore, since we have been justified through faith, we have peace with God through our Lord Jesus Christ, through whom we have gained access by faith into this grace in which we now stand."

Romans 5:1 (NIV)

"In Him we have redemption through His blood, the forgiveness of sins, in accordance with the riches of God's grace that He lavished on us."

Ephesians 1:7–8 (NIV)

CHAPTER 6: SNAKES & SCORPIONS

- Even when the snake is long gone, we recount the story; we gasp about the what if's, and we allow our mind to take us to the deepest, darkest place we can imagine.
- Fear can be maddening, consuming your thoughts and creating anxieties that may never come to pass.
- Have you ever focused on a problem that

became so big in your mind that it consumed every thought, word, and action of your life? Did you come out the other side of that season realizing that your fear of the *what-if* was much bigger than the reality of the *what is*? Believe me—I have spent some time in this season, and my worry did not change the outcome one bit.

- As Christians, we are called to be soldiers for God's Kingdom. Whether or not you realize it, you were born into a spiritual battle, and just like any good soldier, you need to know the characteristics of your enemy so you can train and prepare your weapons for the fight standing before you.

- Know your enemy and remember his tactics: confusion, lies, manipulation, and accusation. Be mindful and watch for attacks or opportunities for him to attack you in your daily walk. He is cunning, and just like the snake, he blends in well with his surroundings.

- Satan can mask his attack as hurt feelings, unresolved anger, pridefulness, doubt, shame, guilt, and unforgiveness. If these emotions are allowed to sit and simmer inside you, Satan can gain a stronghold and begin planting seeds of bitterness in the soil of your heart. He will water those seeds with self-reliance, confusion, and condemnation that can drive a wedge into your relationships and result in you turning away from God's plan and purpose for your life.

- Learn to quickly discern any feelings, emotions, or attitudes that are contrary to God's word and take them captive.

"Jesus said, I have given you authority to trample on snakes and scorpions and to overcome all the power of the enemy, nothing will harm you."

Luke 10:19 (NIV)

"We demolish arguments and every pretension that sets itself up against the knowledge of God, and we take captive every thought to make it obedient to Christ."

2 Corinthians 10:5 (NIV)

"God is our refuge and strength, an ever-present help in trouble. Therefore, we will not fear, though, the earth give way and the mountains fall into the heart of the sea."

Psalm 46:1–2 (NIV)

"The Lord is my strength and my shield; my heart trusts in Him, and He helps me."

Psalm 28:7 (NIV)

"It is God who arms me with strength and keeps my way secure."

2 Samuel 22:33 (NIV)

"God made Him who had no sin to be sin for us so that in Him we might become the righteousness of God."

2 Corinthians 5:21 (NIV)

CHAPTER 7: LEANING IN

- I don't want to wander in worry; instead, I want to fly by faith. I don't want to wade through the problems of life constantly on guard for the next blind curve up ahead. But when I wake up each day and make the choice to lead my life from my limited ground view instead of choosing to follow the flight plan of faith, that's exactly where the road leads, *every single time.*

"Trust in the Lord with all your heart, And lean not on your own understanding; In all your ways acknowledge Him, and He shall direct your paths."

Proverbs 3:5–6 (NKJV)

"Before I formed you in the womb, I knew you, before you were born I set you apart."

Jeremiah 1:5 (NIV)

"For I know the plans I have for you, "declares the Lord," plans to prosper you and not to harm you, plans to give you hope and a future."

Jeremiah 29:11 (NIV)

"And we know that in all things God works for the good of those who love Him."

Romans 8:28 (NIV)

"Whoever dwells in the shelter of the Most High will rest in the shadow of the Almighty."

Psalm 91:1 (NIV)

CHAPTER 8: FOUNDATION OF FAITH

"Now faith is the substance of things hoped for, the evidence of things not seen."

Hebrews 11:1 (NKJV)

- Galatians 5:22–23 tells us that *faith* is a fruit of the Holy Spirit.
- In my life, faith is often found at the intersection of fear and desperation.

"The fervent prayer of a righteous man availeth much."

James 5:16 (KJV)

- God heard my prayers of fear and desperation, and He met me at that dreary intersection of life, providing a light—called hope—for my otherwise very dark path.
- When I could see no way—He WAS the way.
- If you cry out to God, He is faithful to meet you at that intersection of heartache and despair and comfort you in a way only He can.

"Let us throw off everything that hinders and the sin that so easily entangles. And let us run with perseverance the race marked out for us, fixing our eyes on Jesus, the author and perfecter of our faith."

Hebrews 12:1–2 (NIV)

CHAPTER 9: FOCUS ON ~~the~~ Your FATHER

- Life can be confusing when the world seems to be crumbling right under your feet. When you're grasping at this and that, just trying to keep from falling into that never-ending pit of fear and heartache.
- I'm sorry that you are walking through the fire or that you cried out to God for a rescue or healing that didn't happen the way you

planned. Friend, that's so hard, and I sympathize with your pain.

- I will be the first to admit that when the pain is so deep that I can barely breathe, the last thing I feel capable of is giving that to God.

- I have found my feelings hurt when I questioned why God didn't miraculously rescue me at that moment, even as I cried out to Him over and over again. What I have learned, though, is that God *was* there. I just couldn't see Him from my current perspective, standing in my Granny's driveway or hiding in my closet, consumed by fear.

- All I could really process at that moment was that I felt powerless to stop the pain train as it barreled through my broken life.

- I couldn't see then what is so blatantly obvious now. My mom, my granny, myself, and countless others were wounded casualties in my dad's spiritual war. In the aftermath, I can see why God sometimes had to just carry me through that darkness.

- As God weaved my story together, responding to choices made by the key players in my life—He placed His people strategically, each with a part to play, to help me in every time of need.

"Even to your old age and gray hairs I am He, I am He who will sustain you. I have made you and I will carry you; I will sustain you and I will rescue you."

Isaiah 46:4 (NIV)

"See what great love the Father has lavished on us, that we should be called children of God."

1 John 3:1 (NIV)

- God loves you so much that He has gifted you His great love in extravagant quantities. Not only has He given you His great love, but He also knows you as His very own child! Do you know what this really means? You are the child of the Most High King.

- The Bible calls us a co-heir with Jesus Christ Himself! Remember this the next time the evil one tries to tell you he has dominion over you. You turn right around and remind him that darkness cannot exist in the light and your Father is the light of the world.

"You parents - if your children ask for a loaf of bread, do you give them a stone instead? Or if they ask for a fish, do you give them a snake? Of course not! So if you sinful people know how to give good gifts to your children, how much more will your heavenly Father give good gifts to those who ask Him."

Matthew 7:9–11 (NLT)

- As humans, we are all flawed. We are all sinners. Sure, the sin of some is more blatantly obvious and far-reaching than others, but we all have it. The Bible reminds us, though, that there is one who is perfect, who doesn't just practice love as an emotion, but who *is* the very definition of love. And the best part is—He is our Father.

- The truth is God's love for us is far better than

anything we can think or imagine.

- The Bible says in 1 John 4:19 that even our very ability to love is only made possible because God loved us *first*.

- We are victimized by our own spiritual battle, and oftentimes we are wounded casualties in the spiritual battle of others in our lives.

- When we find ourselves in that dark place, the only answer is to focus on our Father. Not our imperfect earthly father, but our Perfect Heavenly Father. The Creator of the Universe. The Creator of You!

"For we are God's Masterpiece. He has created us anew in Christ Jesus, so we can do the good things He planned for us long ago."

Ephesians 2:10 (NLT)

"Yet to all who received Him, to those who believed in His name, He gave the right to become the children of God."

John 1:12 (NIV)

- Friend, you are a masterpiece—crafted by the best artist. He knows everything about you—the good and the bad—and He still loves you with a love so intense that we cannot even fully comprehend it.

I pray that you find this reflection chapter to be a helpful resource. I pray that you will find the courage to take the next small step of obedience in whatever God is asking you to do today. I pray that this book has helped you find hope and has increased your faith in your Heavenly Father. I pray that you find the courage to make your story become your testimony. And, most of all, I pray that as we have journeyed through my story together, we have learned some good solid truth to help us "Just Give it to God."

When you need the shelter
of the Savior—

just give it to God.

When you are burdened
and broken—

just give it to God.

When you are worn out from living
a life committed to chaos—

just give it to God.

When you feel like you are failing
in your faith—

just give it to God.

When you are surrounded by
snakes and scorpions—

just give it to God.

When you find yourself leaning
on your own understanding—

just give it to God.

When you find yourself standing
at the intersection of fear and
desperation—

just give it to God.

If your earthly father is flawed—

just give it to God.

Dear Heavenly Father, Most High King, Almighty God,

Thank You for Your perfect fatherly love for me and for whoever is reading this prayer right now. Thank You for Your provision and protection for both of us today and every day. Thank You for the very breath that gives us life. Father, I pray that You would help us to remember when we are walking through the hard days of this life, You are always there. Father, help us to create habits to run to You for the small stuff so that when the storms of life blow our way, we will remember to run to You first before we get swept off our feet. Father, help us to lean into You as sons and daughters lean into and count on their earthly father. Provide the faith we need through Your Holy Spirit to have confidence in Your promise that You have good things planned for us. Give us a thirst for Your Word so that we may draw near to You and know Your voice. Father, help us remember that the answer is always found in just giving "it" to You…no matter what "it" is. I ask this all in the precious name of Jesus.

Amen

FOLLOW JODI ON SOCIAL MEDIA

Instagram: jodikeith_jojos_photo1

Facebook: Jojo's Photography and More

ENDNOTES

1 *The Passion of the Christ*. Directed by Mel Gibson; screenplay by Benedict Fitzgerald and Mel Gibson; produced by Bruce Davey, Mel Gibson, Stephen McEveety; [produced by] Icon Distribution. The Passion of the Christ. Beverly Hills, Calif.: 20th Century Fox Home Entertainment, 2004.

2 "Chaos." *Merriam-Webster.com*. 2023. https://www.merriam-webster.com/dictionary/chaos (14 June 2023).

3 Jeremiah, Dr. David. "Who is Lucifer in the Bible." *David Jeremiah.blog* (blog). (n.d.) *David Jeremiah.org*. https://davidjeremiah.blog/who-is-lucifer/

4 Jeremiah, Dr. David. "Who is Lucifer in the Bible." *David Jeremiah.blog* (blog). (n.d.) *David Jeremiah.org*. https://davidjeremiah.blog/who-is-lucifer/

5 "faith." *Oxford Languages*. 2023. https://www.google.com/search?q=definition+of+faith&rlz (14 June 2023).

6 "apprehension." *Oxford Languages*. 2023. https://www.google.com/search?q=definition+of+apprehension&rlz (14 June 2023).

7 "apprehension." *Oxford Languages*. 2023. https://www.google.com/search?q=definition+of+apprehension&rlz (14 June 2023).

8 Prichard, Bob. "What Is the Meaning of Faith, Substance, Hope, Evidence in Hebrew 11:1?" *House to House Heart to Heart* (blog). *House to House.com*. https://

housetohouse.com/meaning-faith-substance-hope-evidence-hebrew-111/#:~:text=The%20word%20translated%20%E2%80%9Csubstance%E2%80%9D%20comes,%3B%20Hebrews%203%3A14).

9 “evidence.” *Merriam-Webster.com*. 2023. https://www.merriam-webster.com/dictionary/evidence (14 June 2023).

10 National Center on Substance Abuse and Child Welfare. “Children and Families Affected by Parental Substance Use Disorders (SUDs).” https://ncsacw.acf.hhs.gov/. (n.d.) https://ncsacw.acf.hhs.gov/topics/parental-substance-use-disorder.aspx.

11 Looper Johnson, Chalon. For permission to use her name and the story of the impact her family had on my life.

12 “Lavish.” *Oxford Languages*. 2023. https://www.google.com/search?q=definition+of+lavish (14 June 2023).

13 “Bestow.” *Oxford Languages*. 2023. https://www.google.com/search?q=definition+of+bestow (14 June 2023).

14 Robertson Huff, Sadie. “WHOA That’s Good Podcast.” 2018-2023. Podcast, https://www.youtube.com/playlist?list=PLj4daJNDfmZUA67YNj-4DMiurKG-tR6WQ3 [Accessed June 14, 2023].

Printed in the USA
CPSIA information can be obtained
at www.ICGtesting.com
LVHW011636311023
762575LV00007B/135